Library Orientation Series

Number

19 *Reaching and Teaching Diverse Library User Groups*

18 *Defining and Applying Effective Teaching Strategies for Library Instruction*

17 *Bibliographic Instruction and Computer Database Searching*

16 *Teaching the Online Catalog User*

15 *Marketing Instructional Services: Applying Private Sector Techniques to Plan and Promote Bibliographic Instruction*

14 *Bibliographic Instruction and the Learning Process: Theory, Style and Motivation*

13 *Teaching Library Use Competence: Bridging the Gap from High School to College*

12 *Directions for the Decade: Library Instruction in the 1980s*

11 *Library Instruction and Faculty Development: Growth Opportunities in the Academic Community*

10 *Reform and Renewal in Higher Education: Implications for Library Instruction*

 9 *Improving Library Instruction: How to Teach and How to Evaluate*

 8 *Putting Library Instruction in Its Place: In the Library and In the Library School*

 7 *Library Instruction in the Seventies: State of the Art*

 6 *Faculty Involvement in Library Instruction: Their Views on Participation in and Support of Academic Library Use Instruction*

 5 *Academic Library Instruction: Objectives, Programs, and Faculty Involvement*

 4 *Evaluating Library Use Instruction* (out of print)

 3 *Planning and Developing a Library Orientation Program*

 2 *A Challenge for Academic Libraries: How to Motivate Students to Use the Library*

 1 *Library Orientation* (out of print)

(Most volumes are still in print;
the two out-of-print volumes are designated.)

Defining and Applying Effective Teaching Strategies for Library Instruction

Defining and Applying Effective Teaching Strategies for Library Instruction

Papers Presented at the
Fourteenth Library Instruction Conference
held at Ohio State University
7 & 8 May 1987

edited by
Mary Beth Bunge
Ohio State University

Teresa B. Mensching
Director, LOEX Clearinghouse

Published for Learning Resources and Technologies
Eastern Michigan University
by
Pierian Press
Ann Arbor, Michigan
1989

ISBN 0-87650-252-4

Pierian Press
P.O. Box 1808
Ann Arbor, Michigan 48106

Table of Contents

Table of Contents   v

Preface
   Mary-Beth Bunge and Teresa B. Mensching   viii

Articles

Teaching: No Greater Professional Role
   Keith M. Cottam   1

Inhouse Training of Instruction Librarians
   Joan Ormondroyd   7

Producing Library Instruction Videotape: Avoiding the Mistakes of the Past
   Thomas F. McNally   12

Evaluation for Teaching Effectiveness
   Mignon Strickland Adams   13

Teaming up with Classroom Faculty
   Mary P. Key, Victoria Welborn, and David L. Johnson   17

Poster Session Abstracts   29

Advances in Projection Technology for Online Instruction
   H. Scott Davis and Marsha Miller   30

Reexamining the Library Lecture
   Edward D. Starkey   37

Instructive Library Orientation through Interactive Video
   William J. Frost and Chris Pfaff   37

Strategies for Promoting Bibliographic Instruction in a Liberal Arts College and
   a Research University
   Betty Ronayne   50

Library Orientation Workshop for Support Staff
   Pamela Bradigan and Carol A. Mularski   54

Library Orientation for Support Staff: A Bibliography   54

Team Teaching: Enlivening Instruction for Undergraduates
   Margaret Adams Groesbeck and Michael Kasper   55

From Idea to Publication to Seminal Work: Integrating the Concept of
   Research Fronts into Library Instruction for Graduate Students
   Tara Lynn Fulton   55

CAI Drill and Practice for Library Instruction
   Patrick Boyden   58

Beginning Brochures   58
   Judy Johnson

Active Learning Methods in the One-Hour Bibliographic Instruction Lecture
Trish Ridgeway   61

CD-Roomates: Teaching End-Users to Live with New Information Technologies
Mara R. Saule   64

BI for the Remedial Student
Gloria B. Meisel   69

Formative Evaluation as a Tool for Improving Videotapes for Bibliographic Instruction
Diana D. Shonrock and Michael J. Albright   69

The Effective Use of Slides in Bibliographic Instruction
Donna Bentley and Kathryn Moore   71

The Learning Cycle: An Alternative to the Lecture Method of Library Instruction
Janet Sheets   71

Discussion Group Handouts and Sample Materials

from the LOEX Clearinghouse Collection   79

Arizona State University Libraries   80
Library and Learning Resources, California State University
Long Beach   81
Cornell University Library   83
Douglas College Library   84
Indiana University at South Bend Library   88
Miami-Dade Community College-South   90
Eugene L. Freel Library, North Adams State College   92
Ohio State University Libraries   93
Old Dominion University Library   94
Philadelphia College of Pharmacy and Science Library   98
St. John's University Library   99
Fondren Library, Southern Methodist University   101
Penfield Library, SUNY/Oswego   103
Moon Library, SUNY/Syracuse   107
University of California-Los Angeles Library   111
University of Wyoming Library   112
Cornell University   113
Winthrop College   114

Bibliographies

115

Bibliographic Instruction: Recommended Reading   116

Course-Related Instruction   117

Credit Courses in Library Research   117

Mediated Library Instruction: A Loex Bibliography   118

Evaluation of Bibliographic Instruction: A Loex Bibliography   119

Computer-Assisted Library Instruction: A Loex Bibliography   120

Using Workbooks in Bibliographic Instruction: A Loex Bibliography   121

Library Skills Workbooks in ERIC   122

Teaching The Teacher-Librarian: A Bibliography Joan Ormonroyd 1986   123

Participants   125

List of Conference Participants   126

Teaching: No Greater Professional Role

Keith M. Cottam

For as long as I can remember, I think I've always wanted to be a teacher, but times and circumstances have thwarted my course. I still teach when I can--the Brooklyn Public Library Reading Improvement Program in 1964 and 1965, Brigham Young University in the late sixties and early seventies, the University of Tennessee at Knoxville in the mid-1970s, and Peabody College of Vanderbilt University later on. Those were formal classroom opportunities, but interspersed throughout, beginning in the mid-1960s at Southern Illinois University at Edwardsville, were many bibliographic instruction sessions where I began to shape my outlook on "library instruction." There have also been opportunities to teach Sunday School and other church classes, but all these occasions have been sideline activities to the path that has taken me up the library administration ladder. The payoff in income has been high, the higher I climbed, but inside I have never felt entirely satisfied. I have never stopped thinking of myself as an educator--as a teacher--and I miss the classroom and the rewards of touching the lives of those I would teach. My memories of touching lives are vivid.

TOUCHING LIVES

My office in the old undergraduate library at the University of Tennessee was an impressive place. It had paneled walls, a large desk, a floor-to-ceiling sunny window, and an executive washroom. As director of the undergraduate library, I received many visitors, but one stands out.

I don't remember his name. He just appeared

Cottam is director of libraries at The University of Wyoming, Laramie, WY.

in my doorway one day in a denim jacket and jeans and stood there for several moments before I sensed his presence and stood to greet him. I recognized him as a student who had been in an evening class a few weeks before where I had spent some two hours teaching about the wonderful world of libraries. He said, "You probably don't remember me, but I was in that class you talked to. You made a difference in how I feel about this place."

I stood there and felt very self-conscious.

Then he handed me this handsome little pot and somewhat sheepishly said, "I just want to let you know how much I appreciate what you did and thought maybe you might like this. I made it myself."

Somehow I had touched his life and given him new meaning for an old institution. I had made a difference in his values. And most of all, he had responded. But what had made the difference?

In a more recent setting, I had to blink back tears. Tyler is a six-year-old bundle of energy, ideas, opinions, and outbursts. He is one of fifteen children in my Sunday School class, and I was extended best wishes when he moved up from the younger class. No matter, I thought, but I must admit to feeling a little twinge of anxiety.

The weeks passed uneventfully enough. Tyler was a challenge and he required some extra attention, but then there was that day several weeks ago when he did an extraordinary thing. We were sitting in the opening exercises singing songs and listening to stories before going to class when I felt his little hand in my left coat pocket. I reached in myself and found this big piece of cellophane-wrapped peppermint candy. Tyler just looked up to me with an "it's okay" expression on his face. I smiled. And then, with a spontaneity that no one could resist, he reached up with a hug and said, "I like you a lot."

Again, I had touched a life. Somehow I had exposed him to some behaviors or ideas that had made a difference for him. And most important, he had responded. But what had made the difference?

At Vanderbilt, I didn't get to do much bibliographic instruction myself. By then I was into administration and the business of encouraging others in the BI enterprise. I took every opportunity to expound my ideas with anyone who would listen. After all, I had some twelve years of experience by then and felt quite like a know-it-all; somehow, though, the stature of a Sharon Hogan, Anne Beaubien, Tom Kirk, John Lubans, Evan Farber, or Hannelore Rader always eluded me. But a few people did listen to what I had to say, and one day a young woman walked into my office

and announced, "I think we have some ideas and interests in common and I would like to talk to you." Connie Dowell was impressed by a lecture I had given to a class of library school students at Peabody College, and we have since collaborated on a number of projects.[1]

And so another life was touched. She had been exposed to my ideas and found some meaning in what I had to teach. She had attached some value, some significance, to what I had expounded, and she had responded. But again, what had made the difference?

WHAT MAKES THE DIFFERENCE?

Let's examine that question. Everyone here takes teaching seriously--or so anyone on the outside looking in would expect. But I wonder if there are some who are more the ideologue and less the practitioner. I wonder how many are zealously carrying the bibliographic instruction banner, like an ensign, but fail to be a successful part of the heart and soul of bibliographic instruction--teaching. I wonder how often we get caught up in the philosophy, design, strategy, issues, methods, and techniques of BI at the expense of embracing the most important role--teaching. I wonder how often we rush by the foundation of instruction--teaching --and rob ourselves of a certain sensitivity to those we would teach. Teaching: there is no greater professional role, and it demands our subjective attention. So join me in an inquiry of some important precepts and principles.

I am impressed that certain basic principles properly applied shape the success of bibliographic instruction. Like the roots of a tree, they support and nourish what our students see, and hear, and understand. The branches, leaves, blossoms, and fruit that we display as knowledge, skills, and abilities are determined by the kind of roots we sink and how deep they run. For example, if I wish to be successful at teaching the bibliographic organization and use of journalism literature, I must have not only a command of that field but also a solid grounding in librarianship. I must know something about the practice of journalism, about the authors, themes, and philosophies in the field, and about the application of its literature. Then I must couple all that with instructional design and teaching skills in a way that will touch the minds and behaviors of my students.

That's a tall order. And sometimes, no matter what we do to prepare, we will come away from a teaching experience reliving every painful moment. Sometimes, in spite of what we do, our students are not ready for what we wish to teach, or they don't need it, or worse yet, they don't want it.

Have you been there before? The library orientation presentation where the students are more interested in themselves or others in the class than in what you have to say? Or the instructional session scheduled by an English professor because he will be out of town that day? Or the lecture on chemical literature that bears little, if any, relevance to what is required in the chemistry class?

Perhaps some of those problems are out of our control, but let's assume that our students are ready, willing, and able to learn. What will make the difference? From an inspirational little book published by the Faculty Committee on Teaching at Brigham Young University in 1971 come several ideas that I have applied over and over again.[2]

First, the way we expose students to what we know and what we want them to know may make all the difference. That can surely challenge our ability because students have a range of understandings and interests. Some will be motivated; some will not. There will be those who are intellectually superior and able to grasp the deeper meanings of our instruction; a few will struggle. Others will have the advantage of experience in libraries and therefore relate with what we are teaching; for most, the exposure to libraries will be something new. In the balance, we must learn how to deal with all these variations, to relate with each student as an individual. We may have to adjust--using lectures, questions, discussion, or other learning activities to get our points across. The climate we create in an instructional session for intellectual curiosity, the excitement of chasing down information, or just the satisfaction of knowing the basics of library use, are all dependent on the way we open the field to our students.

Second, what is clear to us as librarians may be quite unclear to our students. We must remember that our personal mastery of library science is ours, not theirs. Further, unlike secondary school teachers who are trained in schools of education how to teach rather than what to teach, librarians are educated as specialists in the discipline and must usually continue to develop the skills to teach it. Assuming that, we must match our understanding of the discipline with our teaching skills, as well as with the knowledge, understanding, and experience of our students. As an example of the importance of clarity, consider the nomenclature and jargon we use in our profession. We understand the meaning of serial lists and union lists, bibliographies and biographies, MARC records and COM records, book catalogs and card catalogs, but do those whom we would teach?

Third, the values, both personal and professional, that we attach to what we are teaching will certainly be evident to our students. Values give credibility to the principles we teach, as well as to the bibliography, reference tools, and search strategies we describe. Our values are shaped by our beliefs and commitments, and asking how committed we are to librarianship as a profession may determine just how successful we are in our teaching. We cannot expect our students to attach value to what we are teaching if they cannot appreciate its significance to us and to them.

Fourth, students who respond are telling us how well we are doing. They are telling us that they understand the meaning of our instruction, that it is clear, and that they have made it a part of their feelings and thinking. They are telling us that what we have taught them is viewed as significant and worthwhile and that it has had an impact on their behavior and what they know. Their response may be the best yardstick we have on just how successful our teaching really is.

CONCLUSIONS FROM INQUIRIES AND RESEARCH

My personal experience and practice are very real, but there are any number of reports, articles, and books that address the issue of effective teaching. Most of them plow old ground and leave one with the impression that the conclusions are just common sense. Nevertheless, research findings and public inquiries lend credibility to common sense and experiential evidence, so a few sources are worth citing.

A Nation at Risk (April 1983) examined six areas, including an assessment of the quality of teaching, and recommended, among other things, that the preparation of teachers be improved. The report generated considerable debate about the quality of American secondary education and spawned a spate of inquiries, studies, additional findings, and recommendations for reform. Many of them are related directly to teaching and what makes a difference.[3] Librarians, of course, responded to the report with *Alliance for Excellence* and *Realities: Educational Reform in a Learning Society*.

Another benchmark report, *Involvement in Learning: Realizing the Potential of American Higher Education*, was published in 1984 by the National Institute of Education. The study group that produced the report implied that for teachers to be successful they must get students actively involved in learning, hold high expectations for student performance, and give students adequate assessment and feedback. The report is often cited by other studies and commentaries. For example, at the 1987 National Conference on Higher Education of the American Association for Higher Education held in Washington, DC, the theme was "Enhancing Performance by Taking Teaching Seriously." One paper by K. Patricia Cross (Harvard Graduate School of Education) stood out. She said, "I think we need to begin to talk boldly about teaching for learning,...about what teachers can do to cause learning."[4] She then summarized the findings from the NIE report and other research on teacher effectiveness into three major conclusions:

1. When students are actively involved in the learning task, they learn more than when they are passive recipients of instruction.

2. Students generally learn what they practice.

3. If teachers set high but attainable goals, academic performance usually rises to meet expectations.

Dr. Cross then observed that "there is no argument in the research community that these conclusions drawn from years of study are significant factors in student learning--nor," [she] suspects, "does any teacher question their relevance. Yet researchers consistently find that such common sense practices do not exist in many ....classrooms."[5]

Two recent journal articles that have influenced my practice as an educator and teacher add some interesting personal insights to the more formal debate about teaching. Last summer *Change* magazine published "A Group Portrait," recognizing fifty higher education faculty members for "making a difference." While the author describes six general qualities these people have in common, the unique factor that stands out in all of them is that they "love teaching."[6]

The other piece is from the spring 1985 issue of *College Teaching*, the familiar old *Improving College and University Teaching* dressed up with a new format and title. The authors of "Achieving Excellence: Advice to New Teachers" state boldly that "New teachers, fresh with enthusiasm, deserve better advice than most educational research provides." They also claim that "to assume that students are learning while the teacher is teaching" is tempting but erroneous, and then they describe and document nine practical suggestions for "new teachers who wish to be excellent teachers."[7] I encourage you to pick up both articles and spend some time probing the meaning and significance of what you read.

MAKING A DIFFERENCE--IT'S UP TO YOU

So from my experience and the literature, how to make a difference and how to be a better teacher begins to take shape. But what do we do to make it work for us? Maybe a simple question will lead to an answer: Why do you want to teach anyway? Is it just a job or a personal commitment? Is the commitment to others as well as to yourself? If you have not examined your motives and goals, that is a good place to start to improve your ability to make a difference as a teacher.

First, what are your personal goals? Learn to define clearly what you wish to accomplish in the context of your values and aspirations, in view of your responsibilities and obligations, and on the basis of a realistic assessment of your capabilities. Establish sound reasons and desires for what you want to do. Learn to plan, either as a continuing process in your head, or, better yet, on paper. Lay out a course of action, set deadlines, and learn to manage your time as well as your tasks. Do you need to master a new part of librarianship? Do you need to develop better classroom technique? Do you need to learn how to tell better stories? Or share more humor?

Develop confidence in your goals. Chip away at your lack of self-assurance, whether it is in the classroom or standing before your colleagues with a new idea. Become more willing to take calculated risks and try to reach higher and achieve more each time you put yourself on the line. Be determined. Don't give up. Look challenge and adversity straight in the face. See the bright side and find the positive in all that you do. For most of us, having no personal goals is probably the greatest stumbling block in our lives. When we don't know where we are going, how we want to improve, or how we want to get there, motivation and progress are usually absent and direction is aimless.

Second, the professional degree--the MLS --is not the ultimate in education for teaching; the degree is just the beginning for the BI teaching role. Successful teaching rests on a broad foundation of knowledge, skills, and abilities, including a working knowledge of teaching skills and methods, understanding of the nature of the learner and the learning process, and of the subject taught. The MLS degree equips us with certain knowledge and skills in librarianship; more important, it equips us with a way of thinking and ways of learning to learn about librarianship. It does not equip us to be successful teachers. For that we must be "natural" teachers, or study and practice the role, or perhaps take a degree in teaching, or discipline ourselves to follow through on a personal teacher development program using such sources as the book *Teaching*

Librarians to Teach[8] or the books cited in the winter 1985 issue of *College Teaching*, "Ten Best on Learning: A Bibliography of Essential Sources for Instructors."[9]

Third, it is simply not true that scholars are bad teachers. The teacher/scholar/librarian model should be encouraged because continuing research or inquiry into the teaching/learning process, as well as the discipline and practice of librarianship, is essential to good teaching.

Scholarship is an interesting concept. Set aside the impulse to race ahead to the anxiety-ridden notions of "research" and "publication" and entertain a few related but less threatening ideas. Scholarship is probably the least understood and appreciated role for any professional, particularly librarians pressed by seemingly incompatible job expectations. Backlogs of uncataloged material, lines of students at reference desks, and budgets and time committed to other activities conspire to play against our involvement with scholarly, learned, or research activities. Librarianship is generally a practicing profession, but that does not preclude the need for scholarship. We cannot succeed in any role in librarianship without the intellectual stimulation that comes from scholarship. For us to conduct the affairs of teaching in a BI program or practice at a reference desk requires a commitment to the process of scholarship and the results therefrom which can develop our expertise and capabilities.

What is scholarship? Too often the idea conjures up an image of bending over some kind of advanced study, or maybe you see a frizzy-haired scientist hunched over a lab table, or perhaps a rumpled scholar existing hermit-like in a study cluttered with books and papers comes to mind. But what I see in scholarship and research is an opportunity to pursue an inquiry, investigate an issue, examine an idea, survey attitudes, study behaviors, develop a new system or procedure, or correlate one set of facts and conclusions with another. Any of these scholarly activities may be aimed at the discovery and interpretation of facts, the revision of accepted theories or precepts in the light of new evidence, or the practical application of what is learned. In my view, librarians as professionals have an obligation to carry out scholarly activities involving at least the practical application of new or revised professional knowledge. For example, if we wish to improve in our work as teachers in a BI program, we must actively confront teaching theory and practice, including the examination of our successes and failures if we wish to climb above ourselves, and the confrontation *is* scholarship. The confrontation distinguishes the role of a professional and scholar from that of a classified job holder who does not work creatively and independently. And so ask yourselves some questions: Do you voluntarily retool and upgrade yourself through specialized study or research? Is your theoretical and practical knowledge being kept updated, active, and alive? Are you changing and adapting as the field of librarianship is changing? Do you stay informed of developments in related fields, particularly teaching? Do you share your insights and discoveries with your colleagues?

Fourth, draw inspiration from your colleagues and others. Call it networking or communication, people learn from each other. The most valuable part of this conference may be our informal conversations and association with each other. We learn from our peers, from mentors, and others who set examples; the personal resources for interaction and learning are everywhere. Facts may be learned from books or from life experience, but an enthusiasm and passion for librarianship and excellent teaching comes from our observations of others who practice and teach successfully. Good teachers leave lasting impressions about style and techniques as well as ideas, meaning, and values. We have all been in the presence of teachers who leave us inspired to do better, to try something new, to reach a little higher, and ultimately to expand our abilities. The question is, do you capture your impressions of the way someone teaches a subject, delivers a speech, or leads a group discussion? Do you take notes on the way a story is told, a concept is explained, an inquiry is pursued, or a situation is described? And then do you think about what has impressed you and how it might be applied in your own teaching?

I am convinced that job satisfaction and professional success are fostered through a process of formal and informal communication. Sometimes the most important teaching moments occur after five o'clock in my office when a colleague drops in to just talk. Away from the pressure of performing or "doing our jobs," we can explore ideas and share insights. We can ask questions and give answers unfettered by formal expectations. Such times are most valuable when I reflect on the conversations and learn from the experiences.

Finally, the realities of successful teaching must be recognized. Teaching success is an illusive thing. From one experience to the next we may reach the heights of satisfaction and the depths of confusion. For most of us improvements in our teaching will come through persistent hard work, honest self-evaluation, and a never-be-satisfied outlook. Training and experience, preparation and motivation, imagination and application, skills, knowledge, and attitude all contribute, but success--making a difference--emerges from sustained effort, strings of small achievements, and one step at a time. Some of us think that just because we are good librarians we should be blissfully good teachers of what we know best. But that is just not the case. We worked and studied to become good librarians; how much more must we work to become good teachers?

SOME PERSONAL THOUGHTS AND QUESTIONS

Libraries are a regular part of many lives, but several years ago I learned just how superficial that may really be. A student stopped me after a bibliographic instruction session with a brief comment: "I've visited libraries ever since I was in kindergarten. I know how to find a book and check it out and I've spent hours reading current magazines." Then she made a remarkable observation: "But until your class, I never really knew how to use a library." Again, I had touched a life, made a difference, and she had responded.

So where are you in your development as a teacher? Sometimes a few simple questions are helpful in assessing where we are, and depending on your answers to the following, you may wish to reassess your involvement in teaching.

- Do you have the personal inclination and motivation to teach?
- Do you have the preparation and the talent to teach?
- Are you inspirational as a teacher--do people respond to your teaching?
- Do you honestly evaluate, define, and face the realities of either your successes or failures as a teacher?
- Do you place limitations on your qualifications and abilities, such as academic preparation, personal preparation, goal setting, practice, perseverance?
- Do you make it your business to know yourself?
- Do you understand those you would teach?
- Do you listen to your students?
- Do you teach individuals?
- Do you prepare each lesson or just wing it?
- Do you develop skills such as humor, asking questions, telling stories, using the chalkboard or marking pad, or using an overhead projector?

- Have you quietly and consciously resolved that in teaching, there is no greater professional service, no greater professional role?

NOTES

1. See, for example, Keith M. Cottam and Connie V. Dowell, "A Conceptual Planning Method for Developing Bibliographic Instruction Programs," *The Journal of Academic Librarianship* 7 (September 1981): 223-228.

2. Reed H. Bradford, *A Teacher's Quest*, (Provo, UT: Brigham Young University Faculty Committee on Teaching, 1971).

3. See, for example, National Commission for Excellence in Teacher Education, "A Call for Change in Teacher Education," (Washington, DC: American Association of Colleges of Teacher Education, 1985); The Holmes Group, "Tomorrow's Teachers: A Report of the Holmes Group," (East Lansing, MI: The Holmes Group, 1986); Carnegie Forum on Education and the Economy, Task Force on Teaching as a Profession, "A Nation Prepared: Teachers for the 21st Century," (Hyattsville, MD: Carnegie Forum, 1986).

4. K. Patricia Cross, "Teaching *For* Learning," (paper presented at the Annual Meeting of the American Association of Higher Education, Chicago, 2 March 1987), 4.

5. Cross, 8.

6. Kenneth E. Eble, "A Group Portrait," *Change* 18 (July/August 1986): 21-32, 37-47.

7. M. Neil Browne and Stuart M. Keeley, "Achieving Excellence: Advice to New Teachers," *College Teaching* 33 (Spring 1985): 78-83.

8. Alice S. Clark and Kay F. Jones, *Teaching Librarians to Teach: On-the-Job Training for Bibliographic Instruction Librarians*, (NJ: Scarecrow, 1986).

9. Maryellen Gleason, "Ten Best on Learning: A Bibliography of Essential Sources for Instructors," *College Teaching* 33 (Winter 1985): 8-10.

Inhouse Training of Instruction Librarians

Joan Ormondroyd

Introduction

When I left teaching in 1969 to enter library school, I thought I had left the world of classroom instruction forever. I cannot say that the thought was a liberating one. I had always loved being a teacher, but the 1960s brought with them new issues in education that led me to believe that the kind of teaching I wanted to do could not be done in the context of the standard classroom. In my search for more relevancy in what I was teaching, I somehow made my way along the path toward libraries. It seemed to me then, as it does to me sixteen years later, that in the free access books and other sources of information lie the real answers to life's questions.

I was somewhat appalled, therefore, upon leaving the University of California, to discover that there were an awful lot of people out there in what is euphemistically called "the real world" who either didn't much care about the answers to life's questions, or worse yet, didn't know that life was asking any to begin with. Forgetting for the moment my own pre-library school illiteracy, I was also appalled at how many people there were who, even when they asked the questions, had no idea how to go about finding the answers.

For some years I floundered a bit, trying to work through my own confusion about what it was my patrons needed--the quick and ready answer provided by the quick and ready librarian, or the independence that learning how to find the answer themselves must inevitably bring. Even Farber, in a recent article on college libraries, cites Peter Dollard, the library director at Alma,

Ormondroyd is with Uris Library, Cornell University, Ithaca, NY.

who said "academic librarians must, to a large extent, see their role as that of a teacher....we do not answer reference questions, we demonstrate a research methodology."[1] Farber goes on to say, "It is not that teaching is a major activity of all college librarians, but that college librarians must enjoy teaching when the occasion arises."

I had reached the same conclusion, feeling that what I must do is begin to think of myself not only as someone who finds answers to people's questions--that is a librarian--but as someone who provides the means whereby people can find their own answers to their questions--that is a teacher --when along came the bibliographic instruction movement of the early 1970s.

Like so many of my peers of those years, I found it wonderfully stimulating to be able to attend conferences (like the LOEX conferences, for example) where librarians were talking about the need to teach patrons how to use libraries. It was exciting to see more and more articles appear on the subject and to find organizations like the Council on Library Resources encouraging the development of instruction programs by offering grants to get them started. I got caught up in the rhetoric of the time and was, at least for a short while, something of a crank on the subject of bibliographic instruction. I, too, applied for a grant, and, to my delight, got the one I applied for. With this money we were able to hire another librarian to take over my reference position for a year while I planned, and read, and publicized. I prepared goals and objectives, decided on evaluation methods, and finally taught, and taught, and taught. By the year's end, I made over one hundred presentations to classes of all sizes and at all levels, and it began to look to me as though the operation was going to be a success at the cost of the doctor's life.

What I hadn't considered at the time I began this program was that being the lone teaching member of the reference staff would put me in an untenable situation. My colleagues had never taught, and while they were not against the institution of bibliographic instruction, they felt they had no aptitude for participating in the program themselves. I soon came to realize that at least in an institution of any great size, if not in all institutions, a library instruction program can only succeed if there are enough teachers available to provide some relief and feedback for each other. How to make sure that we had those teachers? It was that problem that led me to the concept of inhouse workshops to train interested librarians within our system to participate in our program.

I should probably first of all point out that I am not of the school that insists that teachers are born and not made, nor do I feel that the suc-

cess of a library instruction program depends ninety percent on the personality of the librarian developing and administering the program. I have heard both of those statements made by numerous people, including speakers at previous LOEX conferences. I do believe that some people come to teaching more easily than others. We all have varying talents and the ability to communicate is not a talent shared by everyone. However, given a basic modest ability, a willingness, and an interest, many people, if not most, can be taught to be effective teachers. It is my sincere belief that any administration that asks its librarians to administer or take part in a library instruction program, must also take the responsibility for providing those librarians with enough training to enable them to feel comfortable and secure in the teaching role. There is no point, in my opinion, in bemoaning the fact that library schools have not taken on that responsibility. Even if they were to do so tomorrow, there is a whole world out there of working librarians who are in positions where teaching is, or should be, part of their job description and *ex post facto* library courses can do them no good. To wait for library schools to catch up with reality is to put our current programs in jeopardy. Poor teachers do not create strong and successful bibliographic instruction programs. Sheila Creth, in a recent essay, suggests that the university must accept as a primary responsibility and objective, the continual development and training of its staff. "University librarians must demand as much from their libraries in training and development as they demand from library school."[2] I would like to say "amen" to that and add that I think the same should hold true for public and school libraries as well. I believe that inhouse training is practical, essential, and doable and I plan to spend the rest of my time with you suggesting some ways in which you can create such training programs in your own institutions.

It seems to me that there are several approaches that one might take in training staff to be good teachers.

The approach that I have found most successful over the past ten years involves a two-step process: the first step requires the setting up of an inhouse workshop designed to introduce basic teaching techniques to a group of librarians and the second requires careful monitoring of each participant's teaching progress. Let me speak to each of these in turn.

First of all, what are the basic components of an inhouse teaching workshop?

1. **Participants**, of course. A minimum of four persons and a maximum of twelve is what I would recommend. In a 1986 article on this same subject I suggested that participants

should include, in addition to those librarians who need to improve their teaching skills, any staff members whose skills are already very good.[3] For the former group the workshop will be a learning experience, and for the latter it will provide an opportunity to share their knowledge with others--something I believe most librarians enjoy doing.

In some libraries I have visited, librarians from departments other than reference occasionally take part in bibliographic instruction programs. If that is true in your library, you most certainly will want to include librarians from those departments as well. And, as I will mention shortly, you may want to pull in librarians from other libraries on your campus, or from other institutions in the area.

2. **A leader**. Someone who takes charge of the actual program, is responsible for its content, and carries it through to the end.

3. **A coordinator**. This person may or may not be the leader. There must be someone assigned to the nitty gritty task of finding space to hold the workshop, sending out memos to participants, getting necessary clearances, seeing that handouts and graphics are made--the dogsbody work, in other words.

4. **Funding**. This could be major if you decide to bring your leader in from outside of the institution, provide fancy lunches, use lots of heavy equipment, really get carried away. On the other hand, it could be fairly minimal.

5. **Equipment**. If you decide to use videotape in your workshops you'll need tape, a video camera, a playback monitor, and someone to run the equipment for you.

6. **Space**. A training workshop needs room, privacy, and good working conditions. Noisy, cluttered spaces can be distracting and therefore detrimental to the learning process.

Those are the basics. To get your workshop started, appoint a small planning committee whose preliminary tasks will be to find a good leader and to find the money to cover expenses. As I mentioned before, depending on what facilities and personnel you have locally available, your workshop could be either very expensive, or very inexpensive. Generally speaking, the more you can rely on resources within your own institution, the lower your costs will be. At any rate, be sure to work the budget out carefully before you submit it to your administration; administrators like to see the details of a budget before committing themselves to any program. In saying all of this, of course, I am assuming that you work in an institution of some size. For those of you who do not, I would like to recommend that you consider banding together with people from several other institutions who might share your needs and concerns. A small library in a community college, for example, may find that by some careful strategy they can attach themselves to the workshop being considered by a neighboring university. Last year when I gave our annual workshop at Cornell, librarians from a local community college and from a nearby four-year college were among the participants. For those of you who work in large institutions who could handle more participants in your workshop, advertising in state library publications can be one way of opening up the workshop to more people, and by charging a fee, actually raising some of the money to cover costs. The fifteen dollars per person we charged our outsiders last year at Cornell actually paid all of our videotaping costs for the entire session. It was a bargain for everyone.

Once the budget has been presented and agreed upon, it will also be the task of the planning committee to determine who will lead the workshop. The committee will need to write out all of the attributes they consider necessary for such a leader and then begin to look for someone who meets these criteria. Often they need look no farther than their own department, or somewhere within their own institution. If, for example, there is no one directly connected with the library itself, perhaps there is a faculty member in one of the departments on campus who would be willing to take on this task. Good bets are departments of education or communications, or masters of teaching arts programs within various subject areas. I know of one public library that managed to talk several excellent school teachers into helping them lead their workshop. At Cornell, although I like to think that I could handle our workshop myself, I often call on several professors I know who are particularly interested in teaching methods to help me. Not only does this enhance the quality of the workshop, but I think there is something to the fact that no one can really be a successful prophet in his or her own land--even though my professor friends often make exactly the same comments that I would make. The fact that they are from "outside" of our libraries somehow makes them greater authorities than someone who works as a colleague.

The planning committee must also be responsible for setting goals and objectives. Whether the leader comes from outside or from inside the institution, it is essential that he/she be given a clear agenda with which to work. All objectives should be written out in full and discussed with the leader in advance of the workshop. Otherwise you could find your leader and the planning committee working at cross purposes. If there is some hidden agenda that the planning committee or the head of the department would like accomplished, the leader should know that as well. I can tell you from personal experience that it is very disconcerting for a leader to learn, after the fact, that he/she is being used, for example, to help get rid of someone who is seen as a poor teacher. If that is, indeed, one of your hidden goals, let the leader in on it, or it might just backfire.

Another concern the planning committee must deal with is the time when the workshop will take place. Certainly in academic and school libraries the academic calendar will play an important role in determining that date. It is crucial that participating librarians not be distracted by worry about unfinished projects on their desk.

Once dates, budget, leader, participants, and objectives have been determined, the planning committee should appoint one of its number as coordinator to see to the nitty gritty of the workshop: that is, space, equipment, and communication with all concerned.

What the workshop itself consists of has a great deal to do with what goals and objectives have been set for it. There are, however, some basics that I think should be included in any good workshop. All active participants should, in fact must, be required to make a presentation to the group as a whole. This is, indeed, what distinguishes the active from the non-active participants. What that presentation consists of may vary tremendously, depending upon the kind of instruction program extant in your library.

There must be a clear understanding on everyone's part of what makes up good teaching. Rules for good teaching should be discussed at length, and written down, and passed out so that all participants share a common understanding of the workshop's goals.

After presentations have been made, there must be immediate feedback in the form of critiques--certainly from the leader of the workshop--but quite possibly from other participants as well.

And that brings me to what I spoke of as the second step in the teacher training process --namely, the follow-through when the workshop is over. I am afraid that, all too often, librarians feel that once they have held a one-day training workshop, no matter what the topic, the participants will all emerge as newly fledged experts. Unfortunately, unlike most birds who fly as they leave the nest, we need a longer learning period. New teacher-librarians, or those undergoing re-

training, should be given at least a year in which to practice their new skills. It is important that experienced teachers be available to sit in on their classes, and that they be allowed to observe such teachers at work. Team teaching is generally the way I manage to keep an eye on how my new librarians are doing and still honor the teaching commitments we each have. Working with a colleague in the classroom, the skilled teacher can both serve as a role model and observe his or her progress each time a class is given. In addition, sessions for critiques should be held as soon as possible after the class has taken place. Inexperienced teachers need to know what their problems are in order to correct them before they become ingrained. For those trying to unlearn bad habits it will be more difficult, but constant reinforcement from a mentor can accomplish wonders.

Much of what I have said here has been spelled out in greater detail in an essay I wrote last year. It appeared in Alice Clark and Kay Jones' collection called *Teaching Librarians to Teach: On-the-Job Training for Bibliographic Instruction Librarians*, which is listed in the bibliography I provided for your packets. In an effort not to exhaust you with minutiae, I feel that I have kept my comments today fairly general. However, I would welcome the opportunity to discuss in more detail some of the things that were covered in that article, if any of you so desire.[4]

Veering slightly from the topic of this talk, I would like to make one other suggestion that I think is very much related. I am asked quite often, by reference librarians and instruction librarians and by those who perform both functions, how they can make sure that more of their staff in the future will prove able to perform the ever-increasing teaching duties of their departments. As I pointed out earlier, library schools have not really picked up this cue, and all too few of them, even now, are including a teaching techniques component in their curriculum. So, newly trained librarians, with a few exceptions, are not coming into the field with that kind of expertise. I do not, by the way, totally blame the library schools. Given the current, constantly changing technologies, the expected requirements for present and future librarians are massive and unless graduate programs expand to cover a far longer time period than they presently do, there is no way on earth that library schools can possibly provide everything for everyone. Sheila Creth suggests, and I agree, that education for librarianship must be ongoing and that the responsibility for it must be shared among library schools, library administrations, and individual libraries themselves.[5]

So, what I suggest to librarians who ask the question of me, is that they change the way that they recruit their staff and do as university faculty do--require that all candidates for jobs involving public services make a presentation during the job interview. You need not expect your candidate to be a perfect teacher or totally at ease before a group. What you must look for is someone with the potential for those things. What you can spot, even in a raw beginner, are some of the things that go to make up a good teacher. You can spot enthusiasm, self-confidence, clarity of vision, a sense of humor, honesty and tact, flexibility, listening and speaking skills, patience, curiosity, and/or poise. You can also spot severe problems, such as unpleasant voice, odd mannerisms, or confused thinking.

All of this, of course, doesn't mean that you won't have to train your new librarian or that hiring a person with these attributes will preclude the need for workshops, but what it will guarantee is that the training in which you invest will pay off. A librarian with potential is bound, with a little help, to turn into an excellent teacher.

I want to leave some time now for discussion and questions. As I mentioned before, I would be happy to try and address any specific questions you may have, or speak to any aspect of this topic you feel I have not covered adequately.

NOTES

1. Evan Farber, "College Libraries," in *Education for Professional Librarians*, ed. by Herbert S. White. (White Plains, NY: Knowledge Industry, 1986), 55.

2. Sheila Creth, "University Research Libraries," in *Education for Professional Librarians*, ed. by Herbert S. White. (White Plains, NY: Knowledge Industry, 1986), 18.

3. Joan Ormondroyd, "In-House Workshops for Bibliographic Instructors," in *Teaching Librarians to Teach*, ed. by A.S. Clark and K.F. Jones. (Metuchen, NJ: Scarecrow Press, 1986), 82.

4. Ormondroyd, 82.

5. Creth, 18.

Producing Library Instruction Videotapes:

Avoiding the Mistakes of the Past

Thomas F. McNally

Librarians have been producing instruction videotapes for at least twenty years. For the most part, those videotapes have followed the pattern of presenting smiling librarians speaking into the lens of the camera. Occasionally, the tapes have included close-ups of an index finger pointing to parts of a catalog card or periodical index.

The advent of high technology media has produced a generation of sophisticated consumers of media products. Librarians who cannot break from traditional approaches to media production will be faced with video disasters, the worst consequences being an audience that generalizes the library to be as out-of-date as the video they are viewing.

In the past five years, several libraries have produced videotapes that are creative, entertaining, and instructive. Most of these tapes have been joint ventures between instruction librarians and video professionals. It is hoped that the success of this new generation of tapes will convince future library video producers to break from traditional approaches.

McNally is with the Ohio State University Libraries, Columbus, Ohio.

Evaluation for Teaching Effectiveness

Mignon Strickland Adams

"Evaluation" refers to the systematic gathering of information in order to make decisions, decisions that can help us become more effective teachers. Yet the term "evaluation" is one that makes many teachers anxious. To understand the origins of this anxiety, let me begin by examining the two forms of evaluation: summative and formative.

Summative evaluation is the gathering of information in order to make judgments. We gather information in order to make judgments about students--these judgments are called "grades." Information is also gathered about us in order to decide whether we are to be promoted, granted a merit raise, or retained. With such important decisions resting upon our evaluations, no wonder we become anxious.

Summative evaluation can have a number of adverse effects. As stated, it can raise anxiety; all of us are afraid an evaluation may put labels on us we won't like. It can cause fear of trying anything new; if our evaluations are satisfactory, then why should we jeopardize them by trying new methods, which might lead to less satisfactory evaluations. It may lead to denial of the evaluation. Many of us are on campuses where student ratings are required, and have heard faculty members expound for hours on why the use of such ratings is unfair and invalid, even though twenty years of research have shown student ratings to be appropriate measures. Finally, summative evaluation may lead to attempts to subvert the evaluation. When students do this, we call it "cheating." Teachers may do it more subtly, by designing evaluation forms, for example, which measure only

Adams is with Joseph England Library Philadelphia College of Pharmacy and Science, Philadelphia, PA.

their strengths and which give back little useful information for improvement.

Formative evaluation, the gathering of feedback for improving what we do, can have positive effects. We can gather useful information, and we will do it, if we feel that we own the information and that it won't be used against us. For this reason, if the purpose is to improve teaching, then the same instruments or the same process should not be used for both summative and formative decisions. If a librarian gathers information from students in order to improve her teaching, then these results should not be required to be part of her personnel evaluation--although she may decide, if she wishes, to provide either the results, or the fact that she is working to improve her teaching, as evidence for recommendation.

I've said that evaluation can provide valuable information. If that's so, what kinds of things might we want to know for which evaluation can furnish answers? For example, you may be tired of teaching the way you are and want to determine methods of improving. You may be training new librarians and need to have feedback for them. Perhaps your library is facing cuts in staff and budget and you need to justify your program.

These represent just a few good reasons for instituting some evaluation processes. And yet, too few instruction librarians have instituted any kinds of systematic evaluation. If evaluation is important and yields us valuable information, why don't we do it more?

A common answer is "lack of time." We maintain that we have too much to do to add still yet another duty. We may also maintain that the limited class periods we teach leave us with too little time to administer tests or surveys. We also say we don't have these skills. After all, few of us were trained as teachers.

And yet, it is true that we all make time for those things that are important to us. It is also true that the knowledge is readily available in the literature of library instruction as well as in that of education, psychology, and sociology. We probably do not do more evaluation because we are afraid--afraid that instead of gathering useful information, we will be criticized. Becoming a better teacher is a goal all of you share. Evaluation can help you achieve that goal. A major purpose of my presentation today is to show you how evaluation can work for you, and help you take the first steps in your own evaluation program.

When a teacher decides that he wants to gather some feedback, too often his response is to write a test or survey. Before this step is taken, the next step should be to decide what you want to know. The kind of instrument you will choose, and how you administer it, will depend on what questions you want to answer.

One basic question is whether students learned what you wanted to teach. There are several different instruments that could help you answer this question. You could ask the students to actually do what you wanted to teach, which would be a performance test. A performance test sometimes done in library instruction requires students to take a given subject and locate background information, monographs, and articles. An assignment may be a performance test. A research paper tests, among other things, a student's ability to perform the act of library research.

Students may be asked to simulate what you wanted to teach by completing an exercise or worksheet. Or students can tell you on a test or survey what they would do in an actual situation. (Note that students' ability to describe a certain procedure is not necessarily an indication that they will follow it in real life.)

Another question you might want answered is if the material you covered suited student's needs. One instrument you could use to answer this question is a survey. If the survey is completely separate from the students' grading process, they will probably tell you the truth. Ask them, for example, what tools they actually used to complete their project. Another survey could ask their opinion as to whether the materials you covered were what they needed. Responses from their instructors may be useful, although an instructor may tell you whether her needs were met, rather than those of her students.

A pre-test is also a valuable way to determine what instruction students need. A well-designed pre-test can tell you what your students already know. An added benefit is that it can be an indication to students that the library sessions will cover material different from what they have learned before.

Feedback on your presentation skills may be important to you. This may also be done with a survey. However, since students are likely to regard your presentation as a helpful aid (they don't know it's part of your job), their remarks will probably not yield much useful information about areas that need improvement. A new librarian who is just beginning teaching, and who needs reassurance and confidence building, can be helped a great deal by such surveys.

A way to receive useful information is to have a friend sit in on your presentations. This should be a trusted friend--not your immediate supervisor. Having a checklist to use during the presentation can help the friend to identify both your strengths and weaknesses. Representative checklists are available through LOEX. Finally, the faculty member whose class you're teaching can also give you valuable feedback. For example, he may be asked to tell you when you have used jargon only librarians understand.

A very important question to answer is this: is your program making a change in students? One way to find out or evaluate this would be to test both freshmen and seniors. On a small campus, testing all members of both classes can be feasible. On a larger campus, other methods may need to be used. These could include random sampling of students from various levels for tests, simulation of a library search, or responses to a survey. An alternate method on a larger campus could involve a comparative analysis of bibliographies of research papers prepared by freshmen and advanced students.

The second step--deciding what you want to know--is the very necessary precursor of the third step, deciding upon an instrument. When these steps have been accomplished, then you are ready for the fourth step: develop and administer an instrument.

The scope of today's presentation does not allow me to go into detail about developing and administering an instrument. Fortunately, there is a great deal of material available and accessible to you. A good beginning point is *Evaluating Bibliographic Instruction: A Handbook*. Use standard textbooks in education (for developing tests), sociology (for writing surveys), and psychology (for help in program evaluation). Representative examples are listed in the bibliography. You may also consult with a colleague in one of these fields, or take a class on your own campus.

My own procedures for developing any measure can be summarized this way:

1. Write down that you want to know.

    This step is one of the most important ones, and one often overlooked. If you haven't determined the questions you want answered, then the answers you get may be to some other questions.

2. Write objectives.

3. Write the items.

4. Have someone else react to the items.

    For this step, you probably do not want to have a librarian's reaction; he likely will know what you're trying to say. A "naive user," such as a student worker or one of your own children, are more likely to be able to tell you when your wording is unclear or directions are difficult to understand.

    If you are developing a test or questionnaire to administer to a number of classes, you may also want to have an expert react to it--for tests, someone in education or psychology; for surveys, a sociologist or market researcher.

5. Don't explain why your reader should have understood the item correctly; revise it.

    Your goal is to develop an understandable and workable instrument, not to persuade someone that you are right.

After you have gathered information, you are ready for the fifth and final step: USE the information you've gathered. If you have developed instruments that answer the questions you wanted to know about, you will have information that will help you become a better teacher. You will have feedback to improve the content of what you teach, to fit student needs better, and to improve presentation skills.

Your retention, promotion, or tenure will require evaluative information in order to be able to document your achievements. This method will also defend and justify your program.

Information you've gathered can be disseminated in a number of different ways. For example, you may ask classroom teachers to administer post-instruction tests and surveys. Administering the instrument during their regular class will give you more time for library instruction. More importantly, if they administer it, they will also look at it and note comments. Always send the instructor a composite of the results.

Periodically, you can send compilations of evaluations to other librarians and to library and college administrators. While these people are unlikely to look through a stack of class tests, they will be interested in reading one page that summarizes accurately the results of an evaluation.

Articles written for your library newsletter or college newspaper can be made more interesting if figures or quotations are used.

For your own dossier, have another person go through your evaluations and write a summary of the responses. Not only is a personnel committee unlikely to digest a large stack of evaluation forms, but another person's summation is likely to be perceived as more objective than your own.

Always include an open-ended question on tests or surveys. Responses to such questions will be statistically insignificant, and cannot be used to "prove" any premise, but they can be a source of possible quotations, testimonials written in students' own words, which can be powerful statements.

SUMMARY

These are the steps you should follow to use evaluation as a tool for increasing teaching effectiveness:

- First, decide it's worth it. This is the hardest step to take, because you must decide you will take the time and make the effort.
- Second, decide what you want to know. If you don't know where you're going, you're likely to wind up somewhere else.
- Third, based upon what you want to know, select an appropriate instrument.
- Fourth, develop and administer the instrument. Refer to information, advice, and counsel readily available in your library and on your campus.
- Fifth, USE the information you've gathered. You can become a better teacher; you can document your achievements and those of your program.

My topic today has been evaluating for teaching effectiveness. I suggest that it's time to begin.

A BEGINNING BIBLIOGRAPHY ON EVALUATION

Evaluation and Bibliographic Instruction

Evaluating Bibliographic Instruction: A Handbook. Chicago: Association of College and Research Libraries, 1983.
   Designed as an introduction to evaluation theory and techniques for librarians. Contains chapters on goals and objectives, research design, data-gathering instruments, and statistics.

Werking, Richard Hume. "Evaluating Bibliographic Education: A Review and Critique." *Library Trends* 29 (Summer 1980): 153-172.
   An overview of the literature dealing with the evaluation of BI.

Knapp, Patricia B. *The Monteith College Library*

Experiment. Scarecrow Press, 1966.
   Imaginative and useful examples of different evaluation methods are given throughout this discussion of an extremely well-conceived program.

Using Student Feedback

Murray, Harry G. "Classroom Teaching Behaviors Related to College Teaching Effectiveness." In *Using Research to Improve Teaching*, ed. by Janet G. Donald and Arthur M. Sullivan. Jossey-Bass, 1986 (New Directions in Teaching and Learning, #23).
   Puts forth the theory that student ratings of teaching effectiveness can be predicted by the observance of specific, observable behaviors. These behaviors--such as movement, use of concrete examples, praise, statement of objectives--can be practiced and improved.

McKeachie, W.J. *Teaching Tips.* DC Heath, 1978.
   A well-written, practical book on college teaching. Includes a section on student ratings.

Guides to Writing Instruments

Payne, S.L. *The Art of Asking Questions.* Princeton University Press, 1951.
   Although over thirty years old, this is still the most readable and sensible guide to the good wording of questions.

There are a number of basic texts that serve as good guides to construction of tests and questionnaires. Among these are:

Ebel, Robert L. and David A. Frisbie. *Essentials of Educational Measurement.* 4th ed. Prentice-Hall, 1986.

Lien, Arnold J. and Harriet S. Lien. *Measurement and Evaluation of Learning.* 4th ed. Wm. C. Brown, 1980.

Backstrom, Charles H. and Gerald D. Hursh-Cesar. *Survey Research.* 2d ed. Macmillan, 1981.

Teaming up with Classroom Faculty

Mary P. Key

I would like to begin our presentation this afternoon with some background information on the bibliographic instruction program in the School of Natural Resources when I became involved in the fall of 1982. Victoria Welborn will speak to the specifics of our team teaching of Natural Resources 620 and the changes that evolved during the past three years we have taught the class. Dr. David Johnson will conclude our presentation by addressing future plans and how we can improve our teaming up with classroom faculty.

Ms. Welborn and I stepped into an already successful bibliographic instruction program initiated and developed by a Bibliographic Instruction Committee composed of natural resources and library faculty. The library instruction program was based on a three-tiered structure for undergraduates and an advanced structure for graduate students. We just continued that which was already in place as set up by the former agriculture and biological sciences librarians. As we became more familiar with the structure, especially on the upper level (Natural Resources 620), changes were made to reflect the needs of the students as revealed in the evaluations.

There were three levels in the undergraduate bibliographic instruction:

Level One - Natural Resources 100, designed for the incoming freshmen (also included transfer students), had three objectives: 1) introduce students to the OSU Libraries, 2) teach basic search strategy, and 3) provide basic training in the use of the Library Control System (LCS). This was accomplished by the library lecture, a showing of the award

Key, Welborn, and Johnson are with the Ohio State University Libraries, Columbus, OH.

winning "Battle of the Library Superstars," and a library exercise. The library exercise had to be completed in either of the two undergraduate libraries and was graded by the librarians.

Level Two - Natural Resources 201 is an introductory course concerned with resource management problems and their possible solutions. It is designed to provide a foundation and general knowledge in the history, philosophy, technology, and organization of natural resources and their management. The objectives of bibliographic instruction at this level include 1) advanced LCS training, 2) learning definitions of literature types, 3) use and interpretation of the indexes to research literature, 4) learning the mechanisms of citing and annotating literature, and 5) building a bibliography to write a term paper. The teaching format followed that of **Level One**--the library lecture by the librarian and the exercise.

In the fall of 1982/1983 the Bibliographic Instruction Committee, in a review of **Level Two**, felt that the library use concept and exercise should be as fully integrated as possible within the course instead of supplemental as previously taught. The committee also felt the writing of a term paper should be eliminated at this level because it was too much, based on the amount of time it would take in the class. The revised assignments in Natural Resources 201, which was taught in the autumn and spring quarters, reflected the recommendations of the committee and shifted the emphasis from a general approach to a more specialized one to cover the broad interests in natural resources. The students would not be allowed to use the undergraduate libraries, but would have to conduct their research in the Agriculture and Biological Sciences Libraries, and the search strategy would be geared more to their specific subject areas. The librarians presented a lecture on LCS and search strategy in natural resources. Topics were chosen from a list of topics compiled by the committee. The students completed the three assignments as outlined in the class workbook. The librarians were no longer involved in the grading process; this was done by teaching associates. Questions about the library assignment were then included in the final exam.

Level Three - In Natural Resources 620, the objectives included 1) the use of subject-specific indexes, 2) applying search strategy to an intensive library research project, and 3) analyzing and integrating the existing literature. The procedure in 1983 included the library lecture, repetition of the use of LCS, and the library exercises.

As Ms. Welborn and I taught the class we could see the changes that were needed, since the majority of the students had already been exposed to the search strategy and LCS use, either through Natural Resources 100 or 201. There were a few who had to be exposed to Level One--students transferring into the School of Natural Resources, or, those new to the university.

Graduate Level - Natural Resources 785. On the graduate level the emphasis was to apply literature searching strategy to a graduate research project and to conduct an exhaustive literature search. The procedure again was a lecture, and it included online database searching.

The library instruction component of the class was dropped in 1984 due to a change in instruction and lack of funds to support the online database searching. A grant had been obtained to support the teaching of online database searching. When the grant expired we were no longer able to continue. This class also demanded a lot of the librarian's time because online searching was conducted only in the main library and because scheduling the students and working with them in the evenings was time consuming.

The team teaching of Natural Resources 620, which deals only with fisheries management, has enabled us to concentrate on specific areas in our particular libraries and to be better balanced in our bibliographic instruction. Natural Resources 201, which covers all areas of natural resources, has changed from its supplemental status to one fully integrated into the course and is now structured so as to provide a good foundation for proper library use throughout.

Now you will be able to see how the Natural Resources 620 class fits into our team teaching as Ms. Welborn speaks more specifically to our teaming up with classroom faculty.

Key is Agriculture Library Ohio State University.

Victoria Welborn

As Ms. Key has stated, I will be talking about Natural Resources 620 and the changes that have taken place over the years. When the class was first developed, there were two other librarians working with Dr. Johnson. Then, the agriculture librarian left and Ms. Key replaced her. In 1983, I began work at the Biological Sciences Library.

At the time I first began working with the class, there were three library lectures. Ms. Key taught all background and interdisciplinary parts of the library section (i.e., search strategy and LCS, and all the research tools needed) that were available in the Agriculture Library. As biological sciences librarian, I supplemented Ms. Key with the research tools needed by the students that were available only in the Biological Sciences Library. We felt it was important that both of us be present and active in the teaching as they would have to use both the Agriculture and Biological Sciences Library to complete their library research for the term paper.

There are two sets of library assignments. In the first set, students choose a topic for a term paper. First, they must turn in a bibliography on the topic, and later, a term paper. These assignments are graded by Dr. Johnson. The other set of library assignments consists of library exercises, which are done in the library and graded by the librarians. In your folder, we have included a set of the library assignments, both old and new. By looking at the library exercises and the changes that have been made in them, you can pretty well see the changes that have taken place in the class over the past several years.

In 1984, the library exercises consisted of a detailed log titled "Search Log Instructions" (in your packet), and a LCS exercise, titled "Library Exercise." The search log was designed for several purposes. First of all, it directs the student through the process of library research, helping him to apply the search strategy to his specific topic. Secondly, it forced the student to document how he did find information. And, thirdly, it provided the instructors with feedback on the tools that the students used and found most useful. There were some problems with the original log --it was quite long. And as we all know, there are times the search strategy works better than others, or students may start their library research at different levels. We felt there were times when the search log became "busy work" to the student, not an aid, but something he must complete for credit. For example, students often came to the library prepared with the background information they needed, or, the standard tools for background information were not useful. They may not have known what background information they did need until they began looking in the periodical indexes. For these reasons we modified the log assignment. The log currently being used is in your packet titled "Library Log/Pathfinder." This is a shorter assignment. The students are still asked about background information and the types of sources they used. They are also asked where they found journal article citations and which indexes were the most useful. This section continues to provide essential feedback and evaluation to the instruc-

tors. For example, one year we observed that several students discovered government documents and used them as sources. Because of this, we began to include a section on government documents and how to find them in our presentation.

We also changed the approach to grading the logs. At first, we assigned a certain number of points to each question, so a student could make any percent on the log--perhaps eighty percent or ninety-five percent. Currently, we are grading the log as "done" or "not done." If it appears the student has answered all the questions in good faith, then full credit is given. We do not grade the student on the method, just the documentation of that method.

The second original library exercise was the LCS exercise. In the beginning, we also graded this on a point basis. At this time, LCS instruction was included during the class period. We then decided to grade the LCS test like the log, but required each student to make eighty percent on the LCS exercise. If they did not pass competency, then the exercise was returned to them, and they could try again. Soon, student evaluations began to reflect that they did not need LCS training at this level. They felt the LCS training they had had in previous classes was adequate, and we were just forcing them to complete an assignment. Because of this, we dropped LCS instruction from the lecture, and no longer require the assignment. We do pass out the schedule for the LCS workshops that are open to anyone, just in case a student would like to attend.

At the time we revised the log, we felt that the assignments were still not exposing the students to all we felt was needed. A student could complete all assignments very well, without actually handling all the tools. It was conceivable that a student would complete the library section of the course without ever using *Biological Abstracts* or *Aquatic Sciences and Fisheries Abstracts*. As many of the complex tools offer several approaches to information, it was also very possible to use a tool incompletely, not realizing its full power. For example, one could use *Science Citation Index* for citation indexing, and never realize that a free-text subject approach is also possible. We then decided to develop exercises that demonstrated the usage of specific tools. First, we looked at all the sources that we mentioned. We then looked for tools that we judged were both difficult to use and essential. If a tool was judged not difficult to use, such as *Biological and Agricultural Index*, we did not develop an exercise. Also, as there were several Cambridge services mentioned, we decided to only use one for an exercise, since what was learned by using *Aquatic Sciences and Fisheries Abstracts* could be transferred to *Ecology Abstracts*. On the first three pages, you will see the three exercises we use for specific tools, teaching *Biological Abstracts, Science Citation Index*, and *Aquatic Sciences and Fisheries Abstracts*. I do not want to go over each exercise line by line, but in general they are designed so that the student must look at every entry point to information in a source, and also discuss the background information needed to use each source. These exercises are graded on a competency basis.

Thus, you can see that the class is still undergoing revision. As a result of dropping the LCS section, we now only meet with the students for two lectures, instead of three. We have gone from two library exercises to four, yet, we feel that the assignments are more relevant and helpful, without too much busy work.

Before I turn the podium over to Dr. Johnson, there is one more issue I would like to discuss --the advantages and disadvantages to the team teaching approach. To a bibliographic instruction librarian, the advantages are readily apparent. For the student, they have a higher quality of instruction, and more time and guidance to learn how to use the library. Also, when students ask the librarian if they have completed this exercise correctly, the librarian can respond with authority. I know we have all had the experience of guiding a student through a library exercise developed by teaching faculty without consulting librarians where, first, we couldn't understand the assignment either, and/or second, we did not know if this answer was OK because we would not be grading the paper. In a team teaching situation, whatever the librarians tell students in the library will be relayed to the person who is grading the paper. There are strong psychological advantages for the librarian. To have a teaching faculty member recognize your worth and importance at the same level you do can not be overrated. Also, to do a BI lecture a little differently, to be a part of a team effort, and to know a student's name and follow her progress through a quarter is a rare opportunity for a librarian.

But as a head librarian, the disadvantages are also apparent and I feel we would be doing a disservice not to mention them. Both Ms. Key and I are head librarians and the only reference librarians in our libraries. We find ourselves in the position of going out and teaching BI classes, encouraging students to come and ask for help in a library where that help is not always available. I believe you can get some idea of the amount of time and planning two OSU librarians have spent on this one class. This is for the benefit of a class that averages twenty to thirty students, sometimes up to fifty, and is taught once a year. I have several "canned talks" that I have prepared covering the broad areas of biology. I

often find myself giving these talks to classes of two hundred or more. The amount of preparation time is minimal, as is the planning time. These classes are of a lower quality than the class we are describing to you now, and not nearly as personally rewarding. But I do think any good manager and/or administrator must evaluate the quality of a service against the resources it takes and the number served, and what their administration uses for evaluation. In my case, they ask for number served not hours of preparation, nor the quality of the class.

Now I would like to turn the program over to Dr. Dave Johnson, who will discuss the class and its future.

Welborn is Biological Sciences Library at Ohio State University.

David L. Johnson

School of Natural Resources

When considering the question "What changes do you anticipate in your introductory fisheries class in terms of information access instruction?" I found that I hadn't thought as much about the question as I should have. My planning tends to be day-to-day, or, at best, month-to-month. Therefore, I had to do some background work. In the next few minutes, I want to share with you some of my ideas about what factors in our current situation will cause change to occur, followed by some changes I anticipate in our classroom as Vicky, Mary, and I continue to team teach the introductory fisheries management course in the School of Natural Resources.

Students will come into the university with greater and greater diversity of high school experiences. This will be true in spite of recent attempts to unify the entrance requirements of freshmen. The result will be a great spread of language and logic abilities, which will be a challenge to meet using current techniques.

The number of incoming students will be reduced drastically and their choices of fields to enter will continue to grow. Therefore, we will all have a smaller piece of the pie. It will require innovative administration to deal with changes in enrollment in our various departments while maintaining diversity of offerings.

We will see an increasing proportion of nontraditional students including foreign nationals, and more mature students who now have time for an education, or need to retool for changes in their job situation. Their needs and background will be extremely diverse.

There will be many changes in the university that will affect what we do in the classroom. There is a greater reliance by the university on contract research and graduate programs. We now hear that in the area of research only three things 'count': competitive grants, peer reviewed journal articles, and graduate students with completed degrees. The impact on classroom teachers is that there will be less time to spend on teaching, although we see increased emphasis on student evaluations for faculty tenure and salary decisions. As a result, the teacher must become more efficient and effective. As the librarian can help in that process, the classroom teacher's appreciation will increase.

Faculty members change the things they like to do (or are able to do) over time, and the classroom activities change to fit the new style. Computer technology, modeling, and land information systems seem to be the current areas of interest.

The university systems are becoming more automated. Students can now register by phone, and our library system is becoming more and more accessible to remote users. As this phase continues, classroom use of these automated systems will increase.

The university will continue to become more like a corporation. The administrators are going to expect short-term advancements with lots of public visibility. There will be increasing talk of public accountability as the 'ivory tower' continues to disintegrate.

We will also see a change in the 'product' or graduating student coming out of natural resources. These students need to be information brokers. They will need access to large databases as well as literature sources. The emphasis will be on speed, efficiency, and correct answers. Our students will be combining these resources into large computer models that will have good predictive power.

Our students must have the ability to change jobs several times during their lifetime. They will need to be educated, not trained. I also believe, because of the pressures I have discussed, that our field will move more into the graduate arena, and will de-emphasize the undergraduate aspects of our current program.

So, what will the impact be on our class that Vicky and Mary have told you about? I anticipate a change in our goal from "To use the library efficiently and effectively to find, evaluate, and interpret a variety of literature on a particular topic" to "To acquire and integrate information from a variety of sources to make decisions and resolve conflicts." The change may require bringing in more teaching help from other areas, or simply a change in our approach. To effectively teach the variety of students we will have in the future, we will have to somehow individualize the instruction, while still keeping time demands under control. The classroom teachers have other demands increasing at the same time.

I believe we must make more use of computer instruction, while still maintaining the vital personal link with our students that they expect and appreciate. I also believe that we will develop more interactive exercises with our students in the classroom so that they are not so passive in that learning situation.

The future is always exciting and awesome because it is still to be revealed. The key to that future in education is for all of us to work together as a team. If we set up barriers based on our various areas of knowledge, then we will not be led toward integration of knowledge, an absolutely necessary part of future survival. I believe that information science is the key to that integration.

Mary P. Key, Victoria Welborn and David L. Johnson 21

EXERCISES FOR AQUATIC SCIENCES AND FISHERIES ABSTRACTS

Name_____

1. Using vol. 13 no. 11:

If you were interested in the utilization of aquatic products
under what page number would you begin scanning.

There are three entries under "general" for the aquatic products
and their utilization heading. What are two abstracts (give the
number) that may also be of interest but located under a different
heading?

2. Use the cumulated indexes for 1983:

In 1983 ASFA indexed at least one article that dealt with Lake
Erie. On what page of the geographic index can you find reference
to this abstract.
What is the abstract number.
Where do you need to go to find the title and/or authors of this
article.

What is the title of the article?

Who are the authors? By each author's name give the page number in
the author index (1983 cumulated) that reference to this abstract
is made.

Using the 1983 cumulated subject index find a literature review
that deals with catching methods in lobster fisheries. Give the
abstract number.

What information would you use to find the same article in the
taxonomic index. On what page do you find the entry.

From information found in the taxonomic index, what other subject
headings could be used to find this article in the subject index.

Mary P. Key, Victoria Welborn and David L. Johnson: Addendum

EXERCISE FOR SCIENCE CITATION INDEX

NAME_____

Use the l978 Science Citation Index for l978 in the Biological
Sciences Library. Do not use the ones at the Health Sciences
Library.

l. Use the permuterm index. On what columns can you find an
article that deals with seabirds and fisheries. (there are two
columns)

What two authors have written works that deal with seabirds and
fisheries.

2. Look up the entry by R. S. Bailey in the Source Index. On
what page do you find it.

Who is the co-author?

What is the full title of the article.

What is the full title of the journal in which the article
appears.

What volume.   Pages.   Year.   How many references.

3. Use the citation index for l978:

How many works by R. S. Bailey have been cited.
How many authors cited R. S. Bailey.
How many articles cite a l966 article by Bailey that appeared in
vol. 108 of IBIS.

EXERCISE FOR BIOLOGICAL ABSTRACTS

NAME_____

All of the following questions refer to Vol. 75 of Biological Abstracts.

l. You are interested in information on Fishery Biology and Fisheries. Using the Subject Guide found in the beginning of the volume, what concepts or subject headings can be used. Name at least two.

2. Turn to Abstract 2134. What page is this on?
List all the authors, first name first.

Give the full title (not the abbreviation) of the journal.

What volume is the article in?   Page numbers?

Year of publication?   Under what heading or subject area is this abstract in the abstract section?

3. Using the first author, on what page do you find reference to this abstract in the author index?

4. What "background" information do you need to use the generic index?
What is that information for this article?
On what page do you find reference to this abstract in the generic index?

5. List four possible key words that can be used to find this abstract in the subject index.

Using three of these key words, on what page in the subject index do you find reference to the abstract.
Key word_____pg. no.____ _____
Key word_____pg. no._____
Key word_____pg. no._____

Mary P. Key, Victoria Welborn and David L. Johnson: Addendum

6. What type of "background" information is needed to use the biosystematic index.

What page number do you find reference to this abstract in the biosystematic index.

Mary P. Key, Victoria Welborn and David L. Johnson: Addendum

Natural Resources 620
Winter 1987

Name _____

Library Log/Pathfinder

General Topic _____

1. What kind of background information did you need to do your research? What kind of sources did you use to find this background information?

2. What Library of Congress Subject Headings did you use to find books on your topic? What problems, if any, did you have in using the Library of Congress Subject Headings?

3. What years of which indexes did you use to find journal articles? What background information did you need to be able to use each index? What indexes were the most useful and why? What indexes were the least useful and why?

SEARCH LOG INSTRUCTIONS

Title of your topic: _____

Follow the search strategy recommended in class. If you decide to use another method, explain why and describe your method.

As you search, keep a running record of what you are doing on paper. This log will help you plan your activities, tell us what you have tried (even if you found little or no information), and keep you from duplicating work.

Give the following information where appropriate as you work your way through the search strategy. Write down titles, call numbers, etc., as you work.

1. Background Information:

    a. List any dictionaries, encyclopedias, handbooks, reference books, etc. that you used.

    b. How did you locate them?

2. LCS and/or Card Catalog Search:

    a. What subjects, titles, and/or authors you used.

    b. How many items seemed immediately relevant to your topic?

3. Index/Abstract Searches:

    a. What indexes did you use?

    b. What terms, vocabulary, concepts did you look up?

    c. Which terms yielded the most information?

    d. How many items seemed immediately relevant to your topic?

4. Reading and Analysis:

    a. Of the references found in 2 & 3 above, how many items did you actually find?

    b. Of the materials you found, how many were actually relevant? i.e. how many books, how many articles were actually useful?

    c. How many additional references did you find using bibliographies, etc., you located in 2 & 3?

    d. How many of the additional items found (4c) were actually relevant to your topic?

    e. What new terms or concepts did you find to follow-up as you read?

5. Keep track of amount of time you spend searching and record it.

6. What else would you have done if you had had time?

Mary P. Key, Victoria Welborn and David L. Johnson: Addendum

Using the LCS, locate the following giving the information requested:

1. Search for the book <u>Marine Ecology and Fisheries</u> by David H. Cushing.

    Copy all search commands you used to locate the record. _____

    _____

    How many copies are on campus? _____   In which libraries? _____

    Are any copies available for circulation? _____

    Copy the full call number _____

    When was this title published? _____

2. Find other books written or edited by David H. Cushing.

    Copy all search commands you used to retrieve the record. _____

    _____

    How many books by the author are at OSU? _____

3. Display the record for the most recent book by Cushing.

    Copy all the search commands you used to retrieve the record. _____

    _____

    What is the call number? _____

4. Display the Full Bibliographic Record (FBR) for this record.

    Copy all search commands you used to locate this record. _____

    _____

    Who published this book? _____

    Where was this book published? _____

    What subject headings are listed for this title? _____

    _____

5. How many books can you find listed under the subject <u>Fish Populations</u>?

    Use the subject heading listed to find other books on this topic.

    Copy all search commands used to locate this record. _____

    _____

    How many books are shown on this topic? _____

6. Search for books on OHIO fish populations.

    Copy all search commands used to locate these records. _____

    _____

    What is the call number? _____

    Where are the copies? _____

    Do all copies circulate? _____

7. Locate the 1969 edition of the <u>Handbook of Freshwater Fishery Biology</u>.

   Copy all search commands used to locate this title _____

   _____

   How many copies are on campus? _____

   How many volumes does this title have? _____

   Do any of the copies circulate? _____

8. Locate the <u>Journal of Fish Biology</u>.

   Copy all search commands used to locate the record. _____

   _____

   What is the call number? _____

   What year is listed for volume 10? _____

9. Search for the <u>Transactions of the American Fisheries Society</u>.

   Copy all search commands you used. _____

   _____

   Which libraries receive current issues? _____

   When did the journal begin? (Date of first volume) _____

   Does OSU own volume 25? _____

   Explain how you located vol. 25. _____

   _____

Poster Session Abstracts

ADVANCES IN PROJECTION TECHNOLOGY FOR ONLINE INSTRUCTION

H. Scott Davis and Marsha Miller
Cunningham Memorial Library
Indiana State University

Most would agree that the best type of library instruction involves an interactive, hands-on component. Online catalogs in academic libraries present new, yet not insurmountable, instructional problems for BI librarians. There seems to be something very two-dimensional about using the traditional transparency/lecture/handouts approach for instructing library users on how to use an online catalog. Video projection and recent advances in liquid crystal display technology (LCD) provide an exciting instructional alternative to more traditional BI methods. This presentation's purpose is to introduce participants to one of the latest advances in projection technology--specifically, the Kodak DataShow Projection Pad. DataShow is LCD device, which interfaces with an IBM personal computer and standard overhead projector, allowing for projection of terminal screen images as the instruction librarian goes through an actual search. In addition to a demonstration of DataShow, other LCD systems and the SONY Video Projection will be discussed. Positive and negative characteristics of the various systems will be presented.

GENERAL CONSIDERATIONS IN SELECTING
COMPUTER PROJECTION EQUIPMENT

-cost of equipment and any needed peripherals

-portability/storage requirements

-download/simulation capabilities

-durability/warranty

-versatility of applications

-comparative on-site demonstrations of different systems

-satisfaction of other users (request addresses from vendor)

-specifications of room where equipment will be used most,
   i.e., light control, dimensions, power supply, security, etc.

* *

PLUSES AND MINUSES OF THE
SONY VIDEO PROJECTION SYSTEM AND KODAK DATASHOW SYSTEM

The following positive and negative characteristics of the SONY Video Projection System and the Kodak DataShow System have been identified in terms of their utilization and anticipated implementation in the library instruction program at Indiana State University. The extent to which you agree that these characteristics are positive or negative will be determined by the specifics of your library instruction program, and by your intended application(s) of computer projection technology in the program. Given that the utilization of computer projection equipment is relatively new to academic library instruction, this list should not be considered complete.

SONY Video Projection System (Model VPH-722Q1):

+ Capability for projecting "live action" videotapes

+ Well-received by students and faculty; preferred over more traditional teaching methods (transparencies/lecture)

+ Relative portability

+ Maintenance record at ISU is very good

- Cost is relatively high

- Fixed projected image size (7' diagonal max.)

- Sensitive to ambient light; considerable parallax with wide viewing angle

- Magnifies "noise" in live action video images

- Audio quality is only "fair" in live action video

- Diminished image clarity with increased viewing distance

PLUSES AND MINUSES... (continued)

Kodak DataShow:

+ Cost is relatively low

+ Very portable

+ IBM compatible

+ Download/simulation software

+ Unlimited projected image size

+ Less sensitive to ambient light than SONY system

+ Remote control capability

- Fragile

- Image fades when overhead lamp wattage exceeds 360 watts (650 watts
  is the prevalent overhead lamp wattage)

- Software is complicated for persons with limited computer knowledge

- Cannot project "live action" video

- Relatively untested in terms of long-range durability/maintenance
  requirement

- Miscellaneous design "negatives": cabling too short, no "off/on"
  switch on unit, power cord is on the overhead's neck corner.

* *

A NOTE ABOUT OTHER SYSTEMS:

Two other systems which need to be mentioned are the Limelight and the
PC-Viewer, both manufactured by Vivid Systems, Fremont, California.
Our direct experience with these two systems is very limited; however,
each has certain advantages and disadvantages over the other systems
discussed. Promotional literature from the manufacturer has been insert-
ed for the Limelight and the PC-Viewer. When we contacted Vivid Systems
to request the promotionals we found them to be most helpful.

SOME INSTITUTIONS USING COMPUTER PROJECTION FOR ON-LINE INSTRUCTION

The institutions listed below have been indentified as users of video and/or computer projection technology in on-line instruction. The contact persons listed below all indicated that they would be willing to answer your questions or discuss with you their use of the "new" projection technology.

Houston Academy of Medicine......................Contact Person:
Texas Medical Center Library   Dr. Abigail Hubbard
1133 M. D. Anderson Blvd.   Director of Education
Houston, TX 77030   System in use:
(713) 797-1230   Limelighter
                                                Kodak Datashow (in use 1 month)

Health Sciences Library..........................Contact Person:
Univ. of North Carolina   Ms. Fran Allegri
Pittsboro Road   System in use:
Chapel Hill, NC 27514   SONY (ceiling mounted)
(919) 962-0700   [is considering Kodak Datashow]

University of North Carolina.....................Contact Person:
Chapel Hill, NC 27514-6080   Carson Holloway
(919) 962-1151   System in use:
                                                Kodak Datashow

Duke University..................................Contact Person:
William R. Perkins Library   Elizabeth Dunn
Durham, NC 27706   System in use:
(919) 684-2373   Kodak Datashow [not yet in
                                                use; awaiting Toshiba PC]

University of Georgia Libraries..................Contact Person:
Athens, GA 30602   Ms. Deborah Condrey
(404) 542-8460   Bibliographic Instruction
                                                   Coordinator
                                             System in use:
                                                SONY

Indiana State University.........................Contact Person:
Cunningham Memorial Library   Scott Davis
Terre Haute, IN 47809   System in use:
(812) 237-2604, 2605   SONY (in use 2 years)
                                                LCD to be purchased FY 87/88

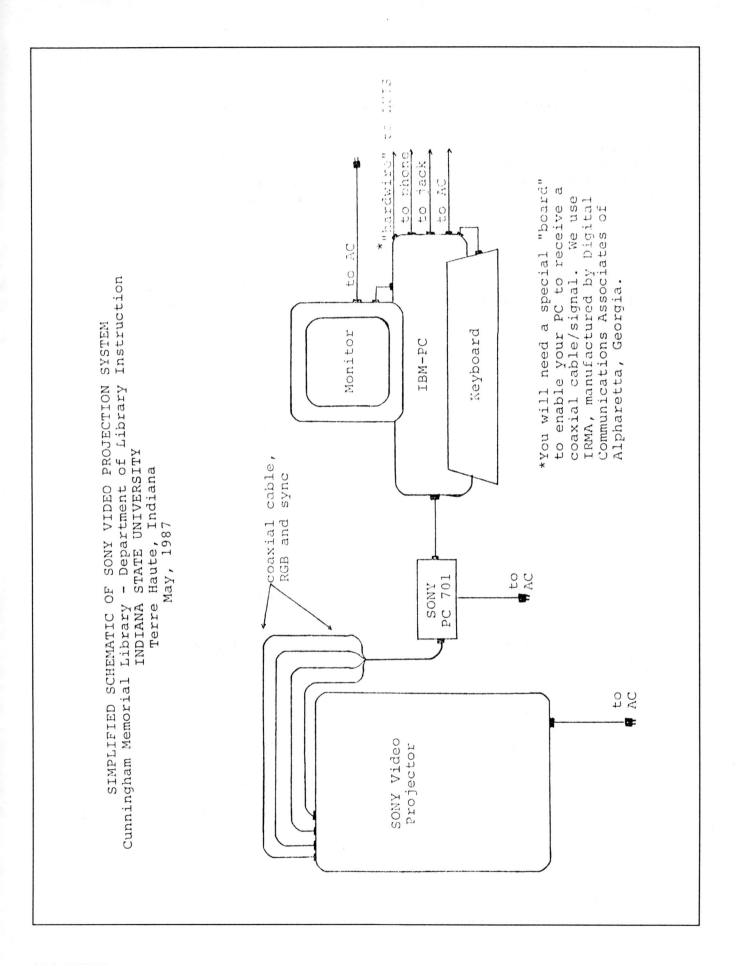

SIMPLIFIED SCHEMATIC OF SONY VIDEO PROJECTION SYSTEM
Cunningham Memorial Library - Department of Library Instruction
INDIANA STATE UNIVERSITY
Terre Haute, Indiana
May, 1987

coaxial cable,
RGB and sync

Monitor

IBM-PC

Keyboard

to AC

*"hardwire" to IRMA

to phone
to jack
to AC

*You will need a special "board"
to enable your PC to receive a
coaxial cable/signal. We use
IRMA, manufactured by Digital
Communications Associates of
Alpharetta, Georgia.

SONY
PC 701

to
AC

SONY Video
Projector

to
AC

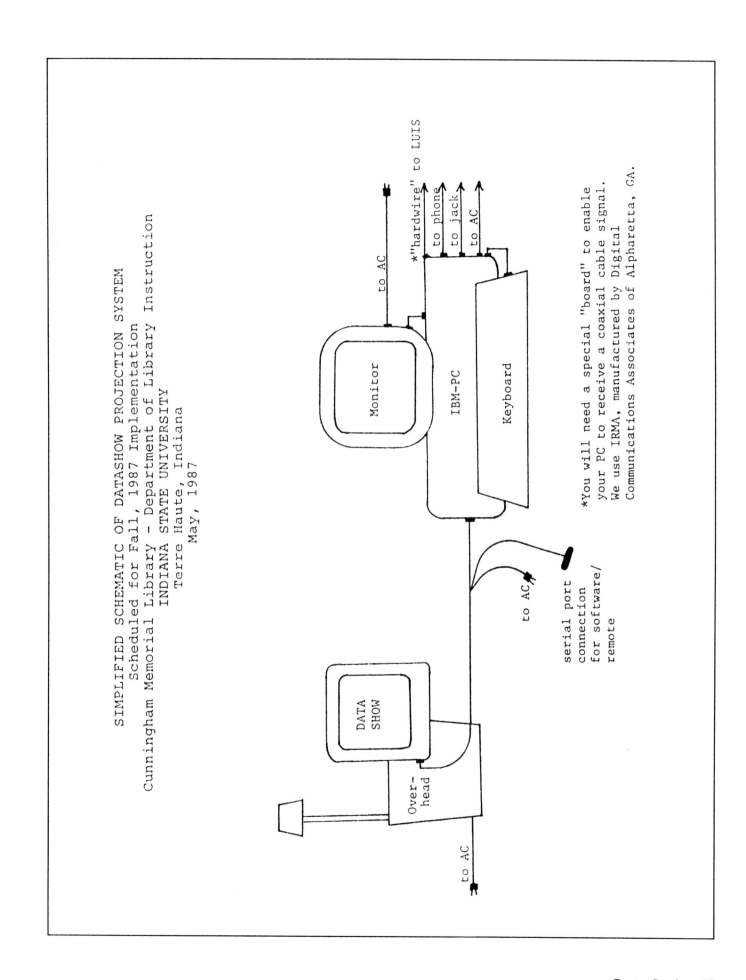

SELECTED SOURCES FOR FURTHER READING

NOTE: While little has been published about video projection as an instructional delivery system, even less is currently available on LCDs.

Anonymous. "Large Screen Data Projection for Computer Classes." T.H.E. Journal, 13 (September, 1985): 74.

Anonymous. "Projection Brings Interactive Video to Computer Classes." T.H.E. Journal, 12 (January, 1985): 92.

Hayhn, Carl H. "How Things Work: Liquid Crystal Displays." Physics Teacher, 19 (April, 1981): 256-257.

Hubbard, Abigail and Barbara Wilson. "An Integrated Information Management Education Program... Defining a New Role for Librarians in Helping End-Users." Online, 10 (March, 1986): 15-23.

Luhn, Robert (editor). "From the Hardware Shelf: PC World Offers First Impressions of Recent Hardware Releases--Limelight." PC World, 4 (February, 1986): 258-259.

Robbins, Chris. "Cathode Ray Tube Faces Major Challenge from Rivals." Computer Weekly, (September 5, 1985): 28-29.

Saffady, William. Video Based Information Systems: A Guide for Educational, Business, Library, and Home Use. Chicago: American Library Association, 1985.

Smith, Judson. "Should You Be Using a Video Projection System?" Training, 17 (November, 1980): 40, 42, 44.

Wendelin, Colby. "The Big Picture." Infosystems, 31 (October, 1984): 90, 92.

REEXAMINING THE LIBRARY LECTURE

Edward D. Starkey
University Libraries
Indiana University-Purdue University
at Indianapolis

The most important result of a good lecture is that a listener is left with the memory that an intelligent, professional person, completely in command of his or her material, presented a well-organized body of difficult but nevertheless intelligible material. Thus, there are two elements to the lecture: the delivery and the material delivered.

Most of us consider the material to be paramount, but on this front the news is not good. On the average, students who attend library lectures (or any other lecture, for that matter) can be divided into three groups: at best approximately ten percent will remember and internalize every main point; forty to fifty percent will remember some things useful; and the remainder, almost fifty percent, will remember next to nothing.

It is possible that a good BI librarian will actually be successful with all three groups of students! If the presentation is well prepared and delivered, even those students who remember nothing of the material will still remember having been impressed by the librarian. This, at least, lowers the psychological price they pay in asking for help.

To arrive at success with all three groups of students, the librarian must give a holistic presentation in which all the elements of good speech are integrated. Visual devices, such as overhead and slide projectors, blackboards, and an occasional book or periodical as an example, are essential. Yet, these must never be used by the librarian or perceived by the students as ends in themselves. All devices are subordinate to the librarian lecturer--indeed they should be understood as extending the power of the speaker to present the material well.

The impact of the librarian is as important as the actual material being presented. Such factors as dress, voice, physical position, and body language come into play. Evident command of material is essential; notes should be used most sparingly or not at all. Direct visual contact with the students must always be maintained; the lights should never be completely turned out when an overhead or slide projector is being used. The librarian should remain in front of the students, should stand, and should move back and forth before the class.

The model for the bibliographic instruction librarian is the master teacher who can take material, which many consider not particularly interesting, and organize and deliver it in fascinating lectures.

INSTRUCTIVE LIBRARY ORIENTATION THROUGH INTERACTIVE VIDEO

William J. Frost
Harvey A. Andruss Library
Bloomsburg University

Interactive video is highly regarded as a medium of instruction because it combines the advantage of videodisc with those of computer-assisted instructives. In a library orientation, it allows a new user to view objects as they are seen in the library, to see locations of collections and services on floor plans, and to both see and hear accompanying explanations. The choice of which segments of the orientation are to be activated, their sequence, and the pace at which they are presented can be governed by the user. Done in this manner, basic instruction can be added to the orientation without overburdening the user. The two chief detractions for I/V--the high cost of producing a single disc and the inability to make changes--can be partially overcome by an inhouse production using eight-inch discs.

LIBRARY ORIENTATION CURRICULUM DESIGN

Statement of need :

     Without an orientation to an academic library, a new user will be at a disadvantage. This is especially so for a first time academic library user, but even users experienced at other libraries may be disoriented since there are many dissimilarities in library practice. Before users can successfully retrieve library materials, they need to know how library materials are indexed, cataloged, classified, and arranged and the location of collection and services within the library.

     Libraries have tried many methods to orient new users: guided tours, audio cassette tours, self guided tour sheets, signage, film and filmstrips (occasionally) and (recently) microcomputer programs. None of these have proved entirely satisfactory because they have not met the following orientation criteria:

Comprehensive
    Need oriented -- Any service or collection can be described when
        needed without the entire orientation being presented.

    Visual presentation of materials and service points with building
        locations.

    No annoyance to other library users.

    Feedback to user of knowledge gained. *

Statement of Goals:

    I. Orient users to the library building and its physical facilities.

    II. Introduce the different collections of the library and their
       locations.

    III. Provide an understanding of basic library research tools and
        their locations:

        A. Card Catalog
        B. Periodical Indexes
        C. Newspaper Indexes

IV. Moniter program use to determine user type, units viewed, time spent, and satisfaction gained.

* (Because of scripting time constraints, no learner feedback goals are included here.)

Program Content:

The program will provide the user with an overview of what the library contains, where things are located, and (in some cases) how they may be used. Contents will include units on building facilities, card catalog use, locating book collections, periodicals and their indexes, newspapers and their indexes, and basic services available to library users.

Behavioral Objectives:

After viewing a unit of the program, the user wil be able to:

1. Locate the facility, collection, or service described.
2. Identify any cards or forms appropriate to the collection on service described.

Instructional strategies:

The user will be welcomed to the program, then presented with a menu from which to select the units described in Program Content. Facilities, collections, and service points will be located by seeing them both in reference to other areas in the building and as indicated in building floor plans. People of different age , sex, and race will be represented using the library.

The entire program can be viewed or, through either menu branching or the program index, only that portion of the program meeting the immediate user needs.

Media selection:

The media selected for presentation of the Andruss Library's Orientation Program is a computer based interactive video disc system.

An interactive video system is individualized, permits a self-paced approach to learning and allows selection and sequencing to be determined by the user. Interactive video disc is used because learning is facilitated by review or repetition of each unit presented and access time is decreased by using video disc over tape. Library resources will be taped in the library to produce a realistic setting.

Hardware: Apple Macintosh Plus Microcomputer
           Panasonic TQ-202YF 8" Video Disc Player
           Sony CUM-1271 Color Monitor
           Assorted Cables**
Software: Mentor Authoring System**
           Mac Video Editing System**

           ** Available from: Edudisc Corporation
                                1400 Tyne Blvd.
                                Nashville, TN
                                           37215

WJF 4/21/87.

Library Project

Level 1 Flowchart

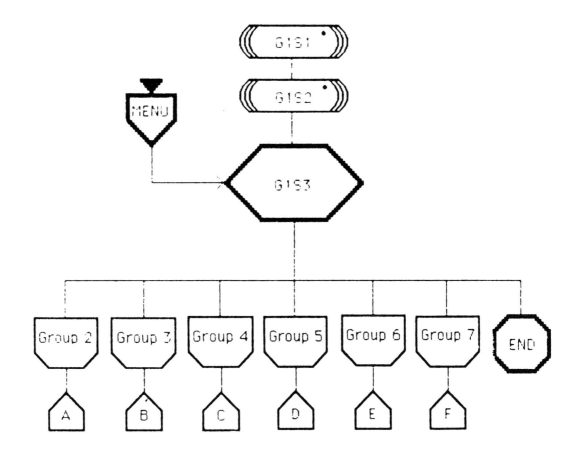

Video	Computer	Audio

G1S1

V-8.23

ZOOM TO EAST ENTRANCE
TO INCLUDE LIBRARY SIGN

[MP-G1S1 -"Library Orientation"]

"THE HARVEY A. ANDRUSS LIBRARY
INTERACTIVE VIDEO ORIENTATION"

PAUSE FOR CLIP (10 SEC)

A-6.68   AUD. CHAN = 2
"Welcome to the Harvey A. Andruss
Library and thank you for taking the
time to view this orientation. We
think it will be time well spent."

___

G1S2

V-4.27

ZOOM TO WEST ENTRANCE
TO INCLUDE LIBRARY SIGN
FREEZE LAST FRAME (FF)

A-2.68

"Select the unit you wish to see
within this orientation program."

___

G1S3

[EXCURSION]

"MAIN MENU -"Click" on the small
box beside the selection you prefer.
Building Facilities
Books: Using the Catalog
Locating Books
Periodicals
Newspapers
Library Services
Index of Subjects
Stop the Course"

PRESENTING
THE HARVEY A. ANDRUSS LIBRARY
INTERACTIVE VIDEO ORIENTATION

Library Project
Level 2 Flowchart

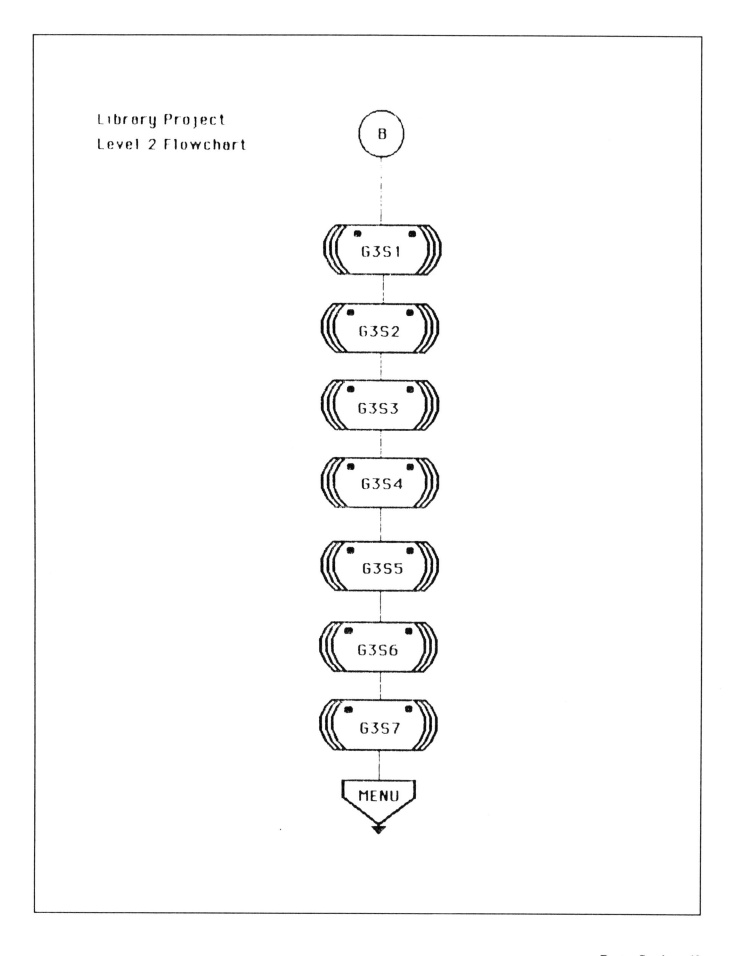

	Video	Computer	Audio

G3S0

BLACK SCREEN

[MP-G3S0 -"Main Menu Selection -
Books & The Library Catalog"]
HOLD 6 SEC

G3S1

V-15.97
PAN OF CATALOG FROM
READER'S SERVICES DESK

FF

[MD-G3S1 -"Books & The Library
Catalog"]

"Card Catalog"

USER CONTROL

A-10.53
"The Andruss Library holds over
300,000 books and can support
research on almost any topic related
to the university curriculum.
Normally, your first step in choosing
books is to use our card catalog."

G3S2

V-19.53
ZOOM TO DRAWER 564

FF

[MD-G3S2 -"Books & The Library
Catalog"]
"SAMPLE CATALOG SEQUENCE
George, Robert
George, William C.
George and Martha
The George B. Pegram lectures
George Washington
George's Store"
USER CONTROL

A-15.63
"Authors, subject, and titles are in a
single alphabetical sequence by word,
except for the articles 'a', 'an', 'the',
and their foreign language equivalents
at the beginning of a title.
When a word is the last name of an
author, it precedes the same word
when used as a subject or title."

G3S3

V-13.73
STILL IN MOTION OF CIVIL WAR
BOOKS

FF

[MD-G3S3 -"Books & The Library
Catalog"]

"Subject search for 'Civil War'
War
->U.S. - History - Civil War<-
Gettysburg, Battle of"
USER CONTROL

A-12.02
"Begin a subject search of the catalog
by using terms specific to your topic.
If you wanted a book about the
American Civil War, the heading
'War' would be too broad, and
'Gettysburg' too narrow."

Video	Computer	Audio

__G3S4__

<table>
<tr><td>

<u>V-18.43</u>
ZOOM TO LCLSH FROM END OF
STACK 25/26 --
SHOW BOTH VOLUMES.
ZOOM TO C.U. OF PAGE.

FF
</td><td>

[MD-G3S4 -"Books & The Library
Catalog"]
"Library of Congress List of Subject
Headings
Use these two volumes to assist you
in accessing the card catalog by
subject."
USER CONTROL
</td><td>

<u>A-11.0</u>   AUD. CHAN. = 2
"Is there a guide to selecting proper
subject headings? YES. It's called
the Library of Congress List of
Subject Headings. This list indicates
the proper terms for each topic and
related terms as well."
</td></tr>
</table>

__G3S5__

<table>
<tr><td>

<u>V-8.63</u>
(REPEAT OF G3S4)
ZOOM TO LCLSH VOL. 2, P. 2301.
C.U. OF BOTTOM OF PAGE
(VIDEO IN-POINT SHOULD BEGIN
WITH THE ZOOM IN, AND SHOULD
CORRESPOND WITH AUDIO)

FF
</td><td>

[MD-G3S5 -"Books & The Library
Catalog"]
"Organization Development
   See Organizational change
Organizational behavior [BF]
   sa Corporate culture
   x Behavior in organizations
   xx Management
Organizational change [BF]
USER CONTROL
</td><td>

<u>A-6.37</u>   AUD. CHAN. = 1
"You may use any term listed in these
books unless it is preceded by a
single 'x' or followed by the word
'See'."
</td></tr>
</table>

__G3S6__

<table>
<tr><td>

<u>V-10.2</u>
ZOOM TO CARD CATALOG --
DRAWER 1061

FF
</td><td>

[MD-G3S6 -"Books & The Library
Catalog"]
[SAME SCREEN AS ABOVE, WITH
"Organizational Change" CIRCLED]

USER CONTROL
</td><td>

<u>A-10.05</u>
"Once you have determined the proper
subject heading, you may go to the
catalog where that heading will be
found. Subjects are in the same
alphabetical sequence as authors and
titles."
</td></tr>
</table>

__G3S7__

<table>
<tr><td>

<u>V-8.83</u>
C.U. OF SUBJECT CARD FOR BOOK
ON ORGANIZATIONAL CHANGE BY
ARGYRIS (DRAWER 1061)
FF
</td><td>

[MD-G3S7 -"Books & The Library
Catalog"]
MOCK-UP OF ARGYRIS CARD

USER CONTROL
</td><td>

<u>A-12.57?</u>   AUD. CHAN. = 2
"There is information on each catalog
card about a book's size, its publi-
cation date, its references, and a
location code."
</td></tr>
</table>

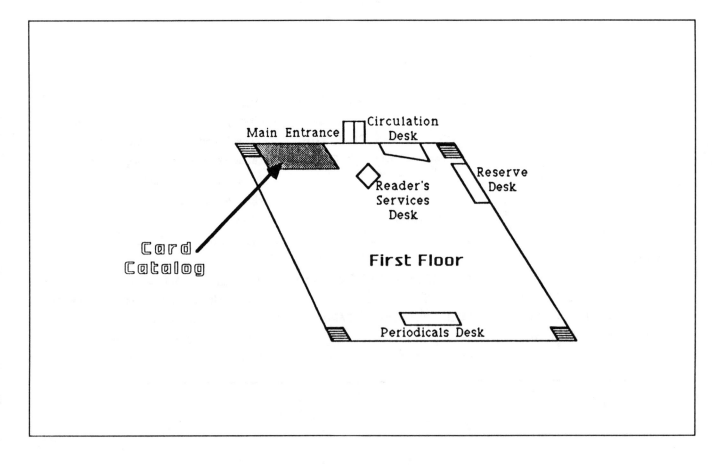

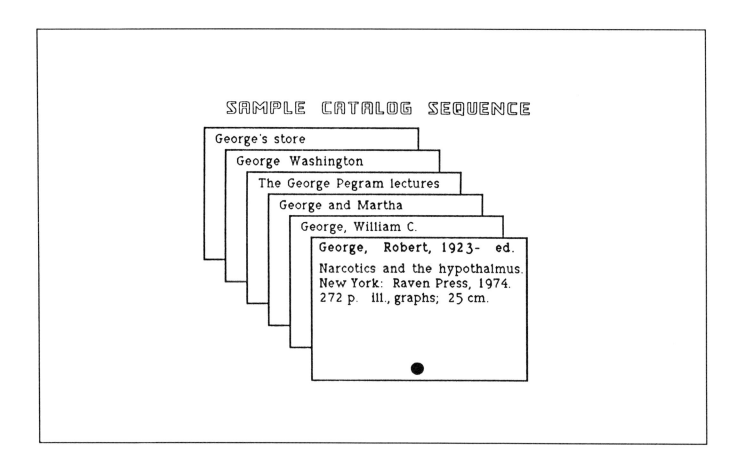

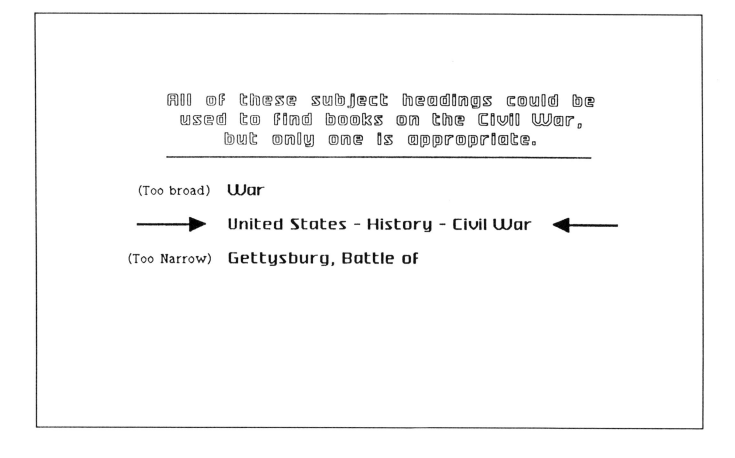

Library of Congress
List of Subject Headings

**Use these two volumes to assist you
in accessing the card catalog by Subject.**

Library of Congress List of Subject Headings

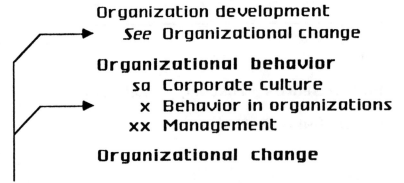

Organization development
See Organizational change

Organizational behavior
sa Corporate culture
x Behavior in organizations
xx Management

Organizational change

Do not use terms followed by the word "see"
or preceded by a single "x".

Library of Congress List of Subject Headings

Organization development
See (Organizational change) ◄

Organizational behavior ◄
  sa Corporate culture
   x Behavior in organizations
  xx Management

Organizational change ◄

Proper Subject Headings.

HD
58.8
.A755
1986

ORGANIZATIONAL CHANGE

Argyris, Chris, 1923-
    Strategy, change, and defensive
routines / Chris Argyris. -- Boston :
Pitman, 1985.
    xiii, 368 p. ; 24 cm.
    Bibliography: p. 357-361.
    Includes Index.
    ISBN 0-273-02328-2

STRATEGIES FOR PUBLICIZING BIBLIOGRAPHIC INSTRUCTION IN A SMALL LIBERAL ARTS COLLEGE AND IN A RESEARCH UNIVERSITY

Betty Ronayne
Eisenhower Library
Johns Hopkins University

This experiential account compares methods of promoting bibliographic instruction at Hiram, a small liberal arts college in northeastern Ohio, and at a leading research institution, the Johns Hopkins University in Baltimore.

Hiram College presents a nearly ideal environment for promoting library services. The mission of the school is excellence in teaching and the 1,100 undergraduates take a core curriculum with a library component required of all freshmen. Librarians have faculty status, serve on faculty committees, and attend faculty meetings. Most of the publicity for bibliographic instruction was directed to faculty and occurred in daily informal contacts. Fliers posted in one or two central locations on campus served to publicize term paper conferences to students.

With ten times the enrollment of Hiram College and 974 faculty, the environment at Johns Hopkins is quite different. Graduate students outnumber undergraduates and all students have a great deal of autonomy in regard to their education. There is no core curriculum and no course that is required of all students. Librarians do not have faculty status, which limits opportunity for frequent contact with faculty members. Encouraging participation in bibliographic instruction requires both a broader and a more concentrated approach. The "target audience" for publicity was expanded to include students and administrators as well as faculty. Mass mailing, stuffing student mailboxes, and postering the campus are some of the methods used to advertise special library events and services. Letters to administrators have resulted in a series of library workshops for graduate students. A letter to the dean of Academic Advising and Counseling has enlisted her assistance in publicizing term paper conferences to student advisees. A special invitation to departmental secretaries brought record enrollment for an introductory library research course. The overall effect of this diversified approach has been an eighty-two percent increase in requests for library instruction services over the past three years.

This instructional session includes slides, examples of letters, and handouts that illustrate different methods of publicity. An eleven-minute promotional video brochure, "Centuries of Knowledge-The Milton S. Eisenhower Library," will be shown.

TO: Faculty and Researchers

FROM: Betty Ronayne, Bibliographic Instruction Librarian

RE: Library Instruction Update, 1986-87

MSEL is changing. This year will mark the introduction of new technology to assist you and your students in library research. Beginning in the fall, a microcomputer will be available in the Reference Department for "do-it-yourself" online searching of many commercial databases. In the spring our online catalog will be ready to supplement, and eventually replace, the card catalog. Computer technology is affecting the ways in which researchers can approach a topic and how they locate information.

What is the best way to keep current with rapidly changing library resources and to help your students improve their library research skills? By participating in our ongoing library instruction program! The new information retrieval systems will be a featured part of our library instruction presentations. Here are a few of the options:

* Library research workshops
* Course-related or assignment-related library instruction
* Basic library skills class
* Special library tours

Of course, a library instruction presentation can be "custom designed" especially for your class. If you would like more information on any of the above, or wish to arrange for a library presentation to your class, please call Betty Ronayne, extension 8366.

THE MILTON S. EISENHOWER LIBRARY
THE JOHNS HOPKINS UNIVERSITY
BALTIMORE, MARYLAND 21218

January, 1985

Dear Faculty Member,

The Eisenhower Library Readers' Services staff invites you to take advantage of a special service: assignment-related library instruction for your students, designed to meet the library research needs of a particular course and a specific assignment.

Here's how it works. After consulting with you on the subject and goals of your research assignment, a reference librarian can develop a presentation of appropriate library sources and research methods. Specific kinds of resources, such as computer-assisted information retrieval, can be highlighted if you wish. These presentations usually last less than an hour and are held in a seminar room in the library during class time. However, other arrangements can be made to accommodate your needs.

Our goal in offering this service is to help students become more proficient in using the library for research. Library instruction related to a specific assignment is immediately useful to the student and should improve the efficiency of research and the quality of the research paper.

If you would like to have a presentation developed for one of your classes, or if you would like to know more about our instruction services, please call me at 8366, stop by the library (Reference Department, M level) or return the form below. Your comments and suggestions are always welcome.

Sincerely,

Betty Ronayne

Betty Ronayne
Bibliographic Instruction Librarian

COURSE/ASSIGNMENT-RELATED LIBRARY INSTRUCTION

Name_____Department_____Phone_____

Course name and number_____

If you wish, briefly describe course assignments or the kind of library research required.

Date: October 27, 1986

To: Faculty Members

From: Betty Ronayne, Bibliographic Instruction Librarian BR

Dear Faculty Member:

Beginning November 3 through December 12 the Reference Department will offer individual Term Paper Consultations for students. Appointments can be arranged by calling the Reference Desk at extension 7773. We would be grateful to you if you would bring this service to the attention of your classes.

We are glad to provide these individual term paper conferences each semester. However, it is also advantageous to present library research information to an entire class at one time. If you wish to schedule time for your class to meet with a reference librarian to discuss library resources relevant to a specific assignment, please call be at 8366.

LIBRARY ORIENTATION WORKSHOP
FOR SUPPORT STAFF

Pamela S. Bradigan and Carol A. Mularski
The Ohio State University
Health Sciences Library

The presenters will discuss the rationale behind the library orientation sessions for secretaries, research assistants, and other support staff in The Ohio State University (OSU) Health Services Center, held in 1985 and 1986. They will also describe the contents of the two-hour sessions, which consisted of detailed descriptions of each library department, a tour of the library, an introduction to the OSU Libraries' online catalog and to medical indexes and abstracts, and the Health Sciences Library's database search services, particularly the contents of and access to the MEDLINE database. The planning of the workshops and materials used will also be discussed.

Two methods used to evaluate the workshops will be described. The first evaluation is a questionnaire measuring the participants' attitudes toward the library instruction, administered at the end of each workshop. The second evaluation, a follow-up survey constructed as an "improvement evaluation," was mailed to each of the participants six months to one year after they had attended the workshop. The results of this survey justify a continued commitment to the library tour and descriptions of departments. The survey results also show the need for the development of a separate two-hour workshop on indexes and abstracts, the purchase of a projection system to demonstrate database searching (including the OSU Libraries' online catalog), and that instructors should take care to eliminate library jargon from their presentations. These necessary changes will be implemented in future workshops for this user group.

LIBRARY ORIENTATION FOR SUPPORT
STAFF: A BIBLIOGRAPHY

Bader, Susan G. "A Library Skills Workshop: One Library's Experience." *Medical Reference Services Quarterly* 3, no. 4 (Winter 1984): 67-70.

Borda, Eva and Mary E. Murray. "Introduction to Library Services for Allied Health Personnel." *Bulletin of the Medical Library Association* 62, no. 2 (October 1974): 373-366.

Gilliam, Bodil H. "Beyond Bibliographic Instruction." *Southeastern Librarian* 31, no. 1 (Spring 1981): 8-10.

King, David N. "Beyond Bibliographic Instruction." *Medical Reference Services Quarterly* 3, no. 2 (Summer 1984): 75-80.

Maina, William. "A Class in Library Use for Allied Health Personnel." *Bulletin of the Medical Library Association* 63, no. 2 (April 1974): 226-228.

Patterson, Thomas H. "Library Skills Workshops for Support Personnel." *RQ* 19, no. 4 (Summer 1980): 351-353.

Poyer, Robert K. "Improved Library Services through User Education." *Bulletin of the Medical Library Association* 65, no. 2 (April 1975): 296-297.

Taylor, Daniel. "Library Orientation for Health Sciences Center Secretaries." *Bulletin of the Medical Library Association* 70, no. 4 (October 1982): 411-412.

White, Donald J. "Orientation Course Aids Staff on the Job." *Canadian Library Journal* 36 (February/April 1979): 17-20.

FROM IDEA TO PUBLICATION TO SEMINAL WORK: INTEGRATING THE CONCEPT OF RESEARCH FRONTS INTO LIBRARY INSTRUCTION FOR GRADUATE STUDENTS

Tara Lynn Fulton
Cudahy Memorial Library
Loyola University of Chicago

What are research fronts? Research fronts are new interest areas in a discipline, which have either splintered from existing research areas or have evolved out of new concerns in the discipline. As the military imagery indicates, they are battalions of individuals who are forging new ground. Code names are assigned to them (scholarly jargon being "buzzwords"), and their progress is carefully monitored. Some research fronts die in the fight, some become the strongholds and bases of new fronts, and others remain as one of the landmark, classic areas of concern that define the discipline.

Graduate students are often called upon to research new topics in their fields. Even doctoral students beginning dissertation literature reviews frequently do not know the historical research base from which their topic has evolved, the tangential fields investigating the topic, or the buzzwords used to describe the topic. Without this background, students find themselves hunting and pecking in familiar indexes and coming up with no information, or with a misleading sample of works on the topic. Unless they have been taught to appreciate the process by which literature in a field develops, students are unable to perceive the holes in their research or the resulting gaps in their understanding of the topic.

An introduction to research fronts and the very pragmatic difficulties they present in the library can provide students with an organizational framework for research and with a more realistic perspective from which to construct appropriate, thorough research strategies. The notion of research fronts can also serve as an advance organizer for discussions on the value of database searching or citation indexes or on a process model for a traditional type-of-tool presentation.

TEAM TEACHING: ENLIVENING INSTRUCTION FOR UNDERGRADUATES

Margaret Adams Groesbeck and Michael Kasper
Amherst College Library

Instruction librarians face two major hurdles when they introduce undergraduates to library resources for a specific assignment in a single lecture: first, let's face it, bibliographic lectures are often boring; second, since the student's experience of libraries tends to vary widely, presentations must be pitched to intimidated beginners as well as to sophisticated users.

Team teaching may be the solution. The authors suggest that two librarians work together, a so-called synergetic team teaching model (distinct from the usual hierarchic team that matches a faculty member and a librarian). Team teaching is better than shouting, the authors insist, and even more engaging than using audio-visual tricks.

Advantage--both in time saved and increased effectiveness--is derived from: 1) shared planning and evaluation, 2) the chance to use different librarians' varied talents for explanation, 3) the increased opportunity to observe audience reaction and apply such observations right away, and 4) the mutual support and encouragement team teachers can give one another. In addition, the theatrical possibilities of role-playing, alternating voices, lively exchanges, and choreography all contribute to keeping students attentive. Team teaching in bibliographic instruction is not just sending two librarians up in front of a class. It requires careful preparation and a sensitivity to the various levels of bibliographic expertise librarians may find in any group of undergraduates.

The authors, who have considerable experience of team taught bibliographic presentations to undergraduates, discuss theory (briefly) and illustrate techniques.

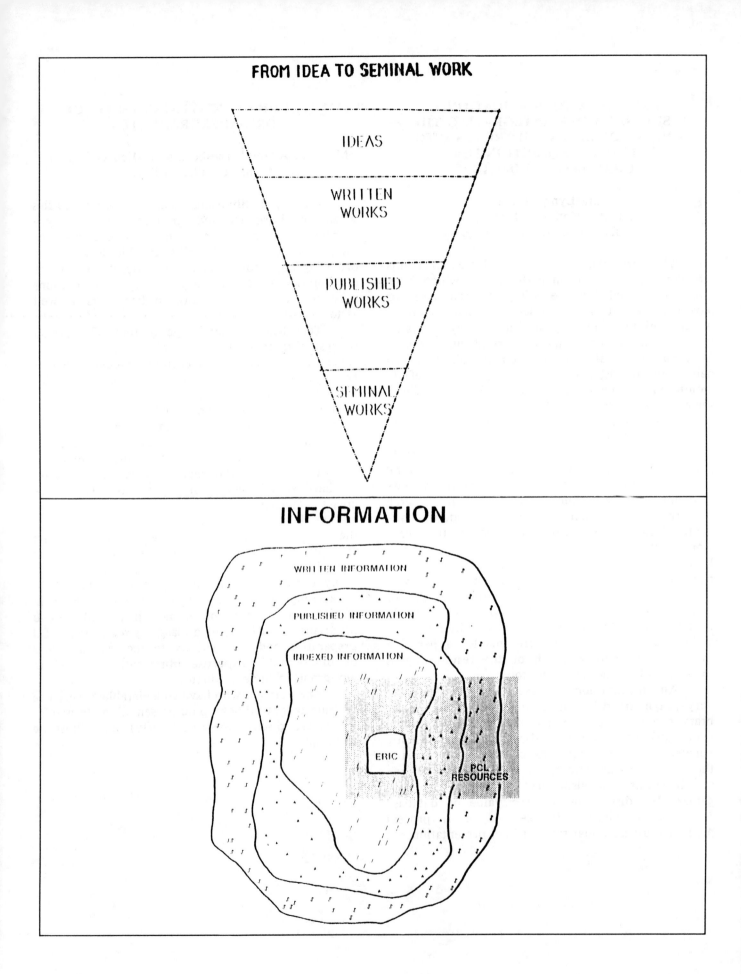

FROM IDEA TO SEMINAL WORK

IDEAS

WRITTEN WORKS

PUBLISHED WORKS

SEMINAL WORKS

INFORMATION

WRITTEN INFORMATION

PUBLISHED INFORMATION

INDEXED INFORMATION

ERIC

PCL RESOURCES

From Idea to Access: The Publication Process

    The following is a list of steps a publication goes through. It represents the point of view of someone who is trying to locate publications such as this hypothetical one. It must be noted that very few ideas ever make it all the way through this process, because there are pitfalls and hangups all along the way, and that's precisely what makes research so much like detective work.

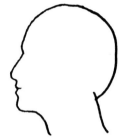

IDEA (known only through personal contacts)

RESEARCH CONDUCTED (listed in newsletters which report ongoing research)

ARTICLE OR BOOK WRITTEN

ARTICLE OR BOOK PUBLISHED

ADVERTISEMENTS APPEAR IN NEWSLETTERS AND JOURNALS

LISTED IN CURRENT CONTENTS OR FORTHCOMING BOOKS IN PRINT

LISTED IN ERIC, OCLC OR OTHER COMPUTER DATABASES

LISTED IN PRINTED INDEXES OR CARD CATALOGS

REVIEWS BEGIN TO APPEAR

CITED IN OTHER ARTICLES AND BOOKS

CITED IN BIBLIOGRAPHIES AND REVIEWS OF THE LITERATURE

CITED IN MAJOR REFERENCE WORKS

ENCYCLOPEDIA Vol I

ENCYCLOPEDIA Vol II

CAI DRILL AND PRACTICE FOR LIBRARY INSTRUCTION

Patrick C. Boyden
University Library
Kent State University

Computer-assisted instruction (CAI) is ideal for instruction in the use of the reference center. The instruction can be used with any individual and is particularly well suited to training reference center assistants employed by the library.

This session will explain the three basic types of CAI lessons: drill and practice, tutorials, and simulations. We will see the distinction between writing programs for CAI use and the far simpler and easier use of authoring systems. Authoring systems for creating CAI lessons are widely available on college and university campuses today. There are systems for use with just about any size and make of computer.

We will cover the most common form of CAI lesson, which is a combination of the multiple choice or true/false drill with the tutorial format. This form consists of expanding the usual curt format to tell why the answer is wrong, reinforce a correct answer, or give some sort of information to help direct the user toward the correct answer.

The card catalogs, indexes, encyclopedias, directories, and others are all collections of facts arranged in specific order and each of these resources has special features to be considered when seeking information for a patron. We will examine question formats that lend themselves well to practice sessions in locating such information.

BEGINNING BROCHURES

Judy Johnson
College Library
Cedarville College

Two groups will be targeted in this session: those just beginning a publications program and those working in small libraries with few resources in terms of personnel and equipment. The importance of clear-cut goals and objectives will be stressed as a prerequisite to design. Appearance of the brochure/handout will be given attention as well. The final segment of the session will touch on typography and production matters.

In dealing with goals and objectives, we will examine the connection between purpose and final product. Three types of print materials and considerations for each will be discussed: how-to-guides and pathfinders, bibliographies, and orientation materials.

Matters of appearance to cover would include uniformity of design, logo and graphics, the use of color, and size of the handout. Examples of various print materials will be displayed to spark ideas.

The last portion of the workshop will focus on actual production. Questions such as whether or not the material should be produced inhouse will be discussed, along with methods of production.

Participants will be given a worksheet to help them with preliminary planning considerations. Reference will be made throughout the workshop to current journal literature, and a bibliography of sources will be provided.

PLANNING WORKSHEET

1. WHY   am I doing this?

2. WHO   is my target audience?

3. WHAT   type of brochure would be
            most helpful?

4. HOW   can I utilize the skills of others
            around me?

5. WHEN   must this be done?

A SELECT BIBLIOGRAPHY ON LIBRARY PUBLICATIONS

Bube, Judith Lynn. "A Coordinated Library Publications Program." _Library Journal_
111 (October 15, 1986): 46-50.

Eldredge, Jon. "Managing a Library Publications Program." _College and Research
Library News_ 46 (December 1985): 620-624.

Hawkins, Marilyn. "A Very Brief Guide to Graphics." _Ohio Media Spectrum_ 34
(Fall 1982): 33-34.

Jackson, William J. "The User-friendly Library Guide." _College and Research
Library News_ 45 (October 1984): 468-470.

Meyers, Judith K. "Useful Publications your School Library can Produce."
Ohio Media Spectrum 34 (Fall 1982): 31-32.

Naismith, Rachael. "Establishing a Library Publications Program." _College and
Research Library News_ 46 (February 1985): 59-63.

§ For Special Consideration: Computer Graphics!

Ammeraal, Leendart. _Programming Principles in Computer Graphics._ New York:
John Wiley and Sons, 1986.

Artwick, Bruce A. _Microcomputer Displays, Graphics, and Animation._ Englewood
Cliffs, New Jersey: Prentice-Hall, Inc., 1984.

Curran, Josephine. "How Computer Graphics can Change your Workstyle." _Public
Relations Journal_ 41 (July 1985): 35-36.

DeWitt, William H. _Art and Graphics on the Apple II/IIe._ New York: John Wiley
and Sons, Inc., 1984.

Simpson, Henry. _Design of User-friendly Programs for Small Computers._ New York:
McGraw-Hill Book Company, 1985.

ACTIVE LEARNING METHODS IN THE ONE-HOUR BIBLIOGRAPHIC INSTRUCTION LECTURE

Trish Ridgeway
Van Pelt Library
University of Pennsylvania

A. Individual Brainstorming, Buzz Session, Group Brainstorming

1. On another sheet of paper, describe in a sentence or two your philosophy of how people learn.

2. Objectives.

3. Individuals will make explicit their assumptions about how people learn.

4. Participants will be exposed to different perspectives and may choose to revise their notion of learning.

5. Individuals will gain an understanding of the use of buzz sessions and brainstorming.

B. Lecture Portion

1. Learning is the responsibility of the learner.

2. People learn through a variety of learning styles. To provide the most people with learning opportunities, use a variety of teaching styles.

3. Pointers for good active learning exercises:
   a. Provide clear instructions through handouts, overhead, or chalkboard including exercise objectives, how to form groups, definite time limits, and who will report back on what.
   b. Insist individuals or groups make notes as they work.
   c. Pick opportunities for active learning carefully--for an affective objective, as an introduction (or set induction), as a review (or closure), or to stress an important point.
   d. Use every moment of the time allotted for teaching activities. Ask professor to stress promptness; have students pick up handouts as they enter.
   e. Plan efficient strategies for dividing into groups by numbering seats, by handing out colored squares or numbers to seated students, or by asking students as they enter to sit only in certain chairs.
   f. Provide students with an opportunity to look at induction exercises while class is settling down.
   g. During group work, circulate among groups to keep students on task and to answer questions.
   h. Make certain students have adequate information to do activities.
   i. Repeat student remarks so all can hear. Synthesize or summarize after groups report.

4. Consult other handouts for additional points such as advantages and disadvantages of active learning methods, examples of techniques and exercises, and selected bibliography.

Objectives:

Participants will remember two most important points of lecture through tie-in to previous group work and through humorous visual hooks.

Individuals will consult information on handouts when constructing their own active learning exercises.

C. Small Group Exercise

1. Form into groups of four to six.

2. Choose a reporter.

3. Begin to design an active learning exercise to convince freshman composition students to use indexes other than *Readers' Guide*.
   a. What is your primary affective objective?
      What is your primary cognitive objective?
   b. What method will you use?

4. Take seven minutes and then be prepared to report back to the group as a whole.

5. Individual groups report.

Objectives:

Participants will utilize the information on the handouts and will gain practice in constructing active learning activities.

Individuals will interact with others in their group to experience the synergism of small group work.

Participants will become enthusiastic about the use of active learning techniques in their own teaching.

Varieties of Active Learning Techniques

Small Groups. Within a single class period groups are usually composed of four to six students who form temporarily to work on a question or problem. Bligh in *Teach Thinking by Discussion* (1986), pp. 2-10, presents an excellent classification of group methods and objectives.

Buzz Groups. Groups of from two to six people who meet for a very short time to review information presented, to formulate questions, to brainstorm, or work on simple problems.

Brainstorming. The instructor invites class members to offer as many answers as possible to a question or problem. Criticism is not allowed.

Individual Task. When time is short, rather than working with small groups, students are directed to work individually on a question and then the group will share their efforts as a whole.

Discussion. The class as a whole discusses an issue or problem. Difficult to get full participation from a group when a guest lecturer. The question and answer technique is a type of discussion. In discussion the problem being considered must be interesting enough to maintain the interest of all.

Advantages and Disadvantages

Disadvantages

Instructor relinquishes control of class.

Students sometimes feel small group techniques are social opportunities and not for serious learning.

Active learning techniques take more class time than the lecture technique.

It is sometimes difficult to get students to participate.

Active learning exercises often take more time to prepare than a simple lecture and may require bringing more materials to the classroom.

Students must have information and knowledge to fully participate in and to benefit from such techniques.

Advantages

Breaks in the lecture help maintain student interest.

Active learning provides students with opportunities to organize and practice information, which results in better long-term memory.

Active learning opportunities within the lecture help meet of needs of students with different learning styles.

Active learning is more effective than the lecture technique for affective objectives (changing beliefs and attitudes) and for higher-order cognitive objectives.

Students enjoy such activities, which gives them a more positive attitude toward libraries and librarians.

Students who work on library exercises in the classroom are provided with a model of problem-solving behavior they should use in their library work.

Active Learning Exercises, Some Examples

Each student receives a sheet with entries from *Library of Congress Subject Headings* and an explanation of the entries. After the librarian explains LCSH, students can work individually or in buzz groups on a couple questions. This also works for such tools as the *ERIC Thesaurus*.

Keep superseded copies of indexes or bring multiple copies of indexes such as Dissertation Abstracts or America: History & Life so students can turn to the various sections as you describe them. If there is time, have buzz groups examine the tool and write a paragraph on how to use it.

Handout an example of a bibliography that might be in a freshman term paper. The bibliography should have a few very good items, several old or irrelevant items, some nonscholarly sources, and overall should rate a D or F by your standards. Have students divide into groups to grade the bibliography and list at least four reasons for the grade they assign.

For a class on locating book reviews, take the end of the period and ask each group to find a popular and a scholarly book review in the book review sources you have brought with you. You have to check out each title in advance; choose examples that illustrate some of the difficulties of locating reviews.

After a presentation on locating subject headings in history or literature, have students individually or in groups make up subject headings for books that yield some representative examples. Hold up books and project copies of title pages on overhead.

As an exercise for closure, give students one or two research questions and ask them to form groups and decide what reference books they would consult for each topic and in what order. Ask questions that demand students consult a variety of sources; for example, "How did Shakespeare differ from the Miles Gloriosus tradition in the character of Falstaff in *King Henry Part 1*?" For a class that is two hours long, each group can be given a different question and then will consult the reference books and catalog drawers that you have brought to the classroom and report back to the group as a whole on their strategy.

As a lecture induction, have students brainstorm to list types of primary and secondary sources of information. The lecture will then take each type and tell how to locate them through the library.

Get a list of student research topics before the class begins. Throughout the class ask students to help out their classmates by deciding on the best periodical index to use for some of the topics, what terms they would use to locate material on others, and the appropriateness of certain reference materials for others, etc.

A pretest is especially useful for subject majors who may feel they have learned all they needed in their freshman library lecture. Some examples of pretests are a matching exercise with reference book types and their definitions, a true-false test on what can be found in the card catalog and what can't, and a test that asks what is the most important periodical index, etc., for your subject field. As a review at the end of the session, students should supply correct answers.

**Selected Bibliography on
Active Learning Methods**

Bligh, Donald, ed. *Teaching Thinking by Discussion.* Berkshire: The Society for Research into Higher Education & NFER-NELSON, 1986.

Bouton, Clark and Russell Y. Garth, eds. *Learning in Groups.* New Directions for Teaching and Learning, No. 14. San Francisco: Jossey-Bass, June 1983.

Cashin, William E. and Philip C. McKnight. *Improving Discussions.* Idea Paper No. 15. Manhattan: Kansas State University, Center for Faculty Evaluation and Development, Jan 1986. (ERIC Document 267 722.)

Davis, Robert H., John P. Fry, and Lawrence T. Alexander. *The Discussion Method.* Guides for the Improvement of Instruction in Higher Education, No. 6. East Lansing, MI: Michigan State University, Instructional Media Center, 1977.

Frederick, Peter. "The Dreaded Discussion: Ten Ways to Start," *Improving College and University Teaching* 29 (Summer 1981): 109-114.

Glaser, Robert. "Ten Untenable Assumptions of College Instruction," *Educational Record* 49 (Spring 1968): 154-159.

Hoover, Kenneth H. *College Teaching Today.* Boston: Allyn and Bacon, 1980.
See especially chapters on questioning strategies and small group techniques.

International Encyclopedia of Education. Oxford: Pergamon, 1985.
See articles by David Jaques, "Group Teaching in Higher Education," and by M.D. Gall, "Discussion Methods of Teaching."

Jaques, David. *Learning in Groups.* London: Croom Helm, 1984.

Johnstone, A.H. and F. Percival. "Attention Breaks in Lecture," *Education in Chemistry* 13 (1976), 49-50.

Lowman, Joseph. *Mastering the Techniques of Teaching.* San Francisco: Jossey-Bass, 1985.

McKeachies, W.J. *Teaching Tips: A Guidebook for the Beginning College Teacher.* Lexington, MA: Heath, 1986.

CD-ROOMATES: TEACHING END-USERS TO LIVE WITH NEW INFORMATION TECHNOLOGIES

Mara R. Saule
Bailey/Howe Library
The University of Vermont

The University of Vermont's Bailey/Howe Library has recently embarked on a unique and challenging end-user search project: a fully subsidized, physically separate end-user search facility that integrates optical, online, and local databases. This facility, the Automated Reference Center, offers patrons access to four optical information sources (IAC's InfoTrac and Government Publications Index and SilverPlatter's ERIC and PsycLit); three online end-user services (Wilsearch, BRS/After Dark, and Dialog's Knowledge Index); and three local databases (our Pathfinder bibliography series, the *Burlington Free Press Index*, and NOTIS, our online catalog).

Although the center is open to all University of Vermont students, faculty, and staff free-of-charge, we do require that each user complete a training program before using any of the systems except InfoTrac and Government Publications Index. Patrons can be trained in one of two ways: they can view a half-hour CAI program on database structure and Boolean logic, followed by completion of a workbook dealing with individual searching techniques; or, they can attend an hour-long workshop, which covers the same information that is in the CAI and the workbook. After being trained, patrons are encouraged to practice searching on the CD-ROM products, ERIC and PsycLit, before they log on to expensive online sources. CD-ROM and other optical information sources afford librarians the opportunity to train end-users in database searching techniques without the cost constraints of logging large numbers of users onto online databases for training, and without the awkwardness of "canned," non-interactive searches on diskette for demonstration. At the University of Vermont, we have found that optical information systems can be effectively used for instructional purposes in the following ways:

1. Training end-users to construct search strategies using Boolean operators and other common searching techniques (nesting, truncation, field delimiting, proximity searching).

2. Using optical information sources as practice media so that patrons become more confident and efficient searchers without incurring large costs.

3. Using observations and written evaluations of optical system use to inform our teaching approaches and techniques for other end-user systems.

Not only are optically based reference sources powerful and cost-effective alternatives to their print and online counterparts, but they also provide the instruction librarian with a new teaching medium that overcomes many of the problems of using other tools for training end-users.

COMPUTERIZED LITERATURE SEARCHING

The Reference Staff of Bailey/Howe Library offers two kinds of computer search services - one that is librarian mediated, and one where individuals may do their own searches (once trained). The do-it-yourself variety is initiated through the Automated Reference Center (ARC), while requests for the service run by reference librarians are initiated at the Reference Desk. In either service over one hundred data bases (generally an automated version of a print index) are available for searching. The advantages of computerized literature searches are:

1. Capability for conducting complex, multi-term searches;

2. Rapid retrieval of citiations from large files equivalent to several years of printed indexes;

3. Ability to adjust or modify search strategy as results are obtained;

4. A printed bibliography, tailor-made, as an end result.

Basic Stategy:

Proper utilization of the search service requires the grouping and manipulation of subject concepts. These operations are carried out through the use of Boolean operators: "or", "and", "not".

Function of specific operators

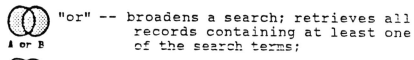

"or" -- broadens a search; retrieves all records containing at least one of the search terms;

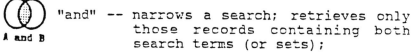

"and" -- narrows a search; retrieves only those records containing both search terms (or sets);

"not" -- narrows a search; excludes those records containing a particular term.

Sample Problem:

I would like to find literature on academic achievement of children of single-parent families.

Concept 1	Concept 2	Concept 3
single parent family	academic achievement	children
one parent family	grades	preadolescents
	performance	
	success	

In order to obtain citations on our specific applications, we want to group synonyms with the Boolean "or" and then combine the concept groups or sets with "and". Of course, you may want to further limit a search to a specific time period of literature, or to certain languages of publication. These and other modifications are possible.

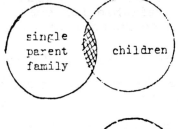

This combination will result in literature on single-parent families and children.

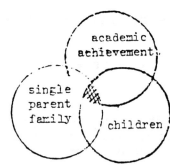

This combination will identify those works that discuss academic achievement of children of single-parent families.

Your Specific Strategy

If you feel your search topic would lend itself to a computer literature search, obtain a "Search Planner" form from the ARC monitor. A reference librarian will be glad to discuss the search strategy with you before you undertake the search, and by all means, do complete the form before you arrive to do the search.

AUTOMATED REFERENCE CENTER
BAILEY/HOWE LIBRARY
656-2924

WHAT IS THE ARC?   The Automated Reference Center (ARC), located on the first floor of the Bailey/Howe Library across from the Reference Desk, is a place where you can do your own computerized literature searching of national and local databases. Millions of journals, books, reports, conference proceedings, dissertations, and government documents can be searched for bibliographic information pertaining to your particular interests. Subject areas include business, social sciences, agriculture, psychology, education, medicine, science, technology, and humanities.

In addition to InfoTrac, the ARC offers you access to two databases on compact disc (ERIC and PsycLit) and three national database services (BRS/After Dark, Dialog's Knowledge Index, and Wilsearch), each providing you with many individual databases to search. Ask the ARC monitor for a list of these databases.

WHO CAN USE THE ARC?   Anyone with a valid UVM faculty, staff, or student I.D. can use these services. Non-UVM patrons can use InfoTrac, ERIC, and PsycLit under the conditions outlined in "Special Guidelines for Use of the Automated Reference Center by Non-UVM Affiliates."

HOW DO I USE IT?   No computer experience is necessary. You must, however, complete an instructional program in the techniques of database searching before you use any of the services, except InfoTrac. To fulfill the training requirement, you can either complete a computerized instructional diskette and workbook, or attend an introductory workshop; ask the ARC monitor for details.

Once trained, you may make a half-hour appointment to use one of the ARC services. Only one appointment per day can be made, and sign-up can be no more that one week in advance. No appointment is needed for InfoTrac. "Walk-in" use of the ARC will be permitted if a station is free and no one else has made an appointment for that time period. Those who have made an appointment but do not show up in ten minutes will give up their time slot.

WHEN ARE THE ARC SERVICES AVAILABLE?
InfoTrac, ERIC, PsycLit, Wilsearch: M-Th 8am-11:30pm
Fri 8am-9pm
Sat 9am-5pm
Sun 10am-11:30pm

BRS/After Dark and Knowledge Index: M-Th 6pm-11:30pm
Fri 6pm-9pm
Sat 9am-5pm
Sun 10am-11:30pm
(BRS/After Dark)
3pm-11:30pm
(Knowledge Index)

HOW MUCH DOES IT COST?

There is no charge to you for any of these services.

BAILEY/HOWE LIBRARY
AUTOMATED REFERENCE CENTER
SEARCH PLANNER

IF YOU WILL BE SEARCHING BRS/AFTER DARK, KNOWLEDGE INDEX, OR
WILSEARCH, YOU MUST HAVE THIS FORM REVIEWED BY A REFERENCE
LIBRARIAN.

1. State your search topic as completely as you can:

    _____

    _____

2. Select the database(s) and service (Wilsearch, BRS/After Dark,
Knowledge Index, ERIC/CD or PSYC/CD) that best covers your topic.
The ARC monitor can provide a list of databases.

    Database(s): _____ Service: _____

3. Think about your topic and circle the two or three most
important different parts, or concepts, above.

4. Write each concept you circled in a top space, then list
synonymous or related terms, if applicable. If a thesaurus is
available for your database, use appropriate terms from it also.

   First Concept   Second Concept   Third Concept

   _____   _____   _____

   OR_____   OR_____   OR_____

   OR_____   OR_____   OR_____

   OR_____   OR_____   OR_____

Connectors: _____   _____

5. Insert the connectors AND, OR, NOT, or others specified by
the service between the concepts above to combine them into a
search statement.

6. Write out the search statements you will enter in order to
get your first sets:

        1._____

        2._____

        3._____

        4._____

7. What command will you use to logoff the system? _____

ASK THE MONITOR FOR HELP WITH THIS FORM AND WITH SEARCHING!!!

BI FOR THE REMEDIAL STUDENT

Gloria B. Meisel
College Library
Westchester Community College

Any bibliographic instruction program must be flexible enough to address many different groups of students. This is particularly true in a community college setting where the non-traditional student is likely to be the norm. One such group is that of remedial (sometimes referred to as developmental) students. They cannot use a library successfully and may often go to great lengths to avoid trying. They may never or seldom have had the opportunity to succeed. To combat the intimidation and previous failure rate experienced by this group of students, college libraries should develop specific programs and/or library assignments to ensure positive academic reinforcement.

The BI librarian(s) must engage in active communication with the department under whose aegis the remediation students are placed. A series of competency-based assignments is one way to promote a positive attitude toward library use based on the high rate of the students' completion of those assignments. Communication is the key word. Communication must be not only between faculty, but with the students as well to identify their needs and fears (such as use of microfilm machines). This talk will center on the evolution of the communication between our college's Learning Resource Center faculty and the Reading Department faculty. It will show the specific assignments and programs that have been successful.

FORMATIVE EVALUATION AS A TOOL FOR IMPROVING VIDEOTAPES FOR BIBLIOGRAPHIC INSTRUCTION

Diane D. Shonrock and Michael J. Albright
Parks Library
Iowa State University

It has been estimated that over six hundred academic librarians have produced videotapes for the purpose of bibliographic instruction (McNally, 1986). Full-scale production efforts to develop such tapes have been described by a number of authors (e.g., Liebman, 1980; Blythe and Sweet, 1980; Nagy and Thomas, 1981; Siegel and McNally, 1983; Jacobson and Albright, 1983; Chiang and Kautz, 1985). Video has been shown to have had a positive impact on students in both the cognitive (knowledge) and affective (attitudes) domains.

Of the publications cited above, only Jacobson and Albright described the application of an instructional design model during the tape development process. Of particular concern has been the virtual absence of any descriptions of efforts in the area of formative evaluation. Formative evaluation is the collection and analysis of data during the development stage for the purpose of identifying weaknesses and making revisions to improve the instructional integrity of the product.

This presentation would describe the manner in which formative evaluation was applied during development of videotapes for bibliographic instruction at Iowa State University (ISU). The project began in 1980 with an extensive front-end analysis of the instructional problem and development of a pilot tape. The pilot tape was field tested with students, and evaluation results were used to guide the design of four videotapes that were produced in 1981. A thorough evaluation of these tapes provided information that was extremely valuable when they were revised in 1985. Examples illustrating specific changes will be shown, and copies of the evaluation instruments will be shared.

Library 160 Tape Evaluation

In the following statement, designate your choice by filling in the proper space.

1. I am classified as a A. Freshman; B. Sophomore; C. Junior; D. Senior.

   Use the following scale to indicate how much you agree or disagree with the following statements.

   A. Strongly Agree
   B. Agree
   C. Neutral
   D. Disagree
   E. Strongly Disagree

2. I was quite interested in using the library even before I took this course.

3. I believe that a course like Library Instruction 160 is necessary for undergraduates to learn how to use the library effectively.

4. The Instructional Manual seems to have a lot of important information.

5. I enjoyed watching these video tapes.

6. I think that these video tapes are worthwhile and should be shown to future Library Instruction 160 classes.

7. An important purpose of the video tapes was to interest me in learning how to use the library.

8. Information in the video tapes was presented too quickly; I had trouble keeping up with it.

9. I understood why the production crew was in the library.

10. The tour, via the video tape, helped me to find my way around the library.

11. Shannon's experience was typical -- the librarians really can help students learn how to use the library.

12. Even though Shannon worked in the library, it seemed that he knew too much about it for his character to be realistic.

13. The humor in the video tapes helped to make them interesting.

14. For the most part, the characters in the video tapes seemed real.

The video tapes demonstrated how easy it is to........

15. .....use the Card Catalog.

16. .....use the Guide to the General Collection.

17. .....find a book in the stacks.

18. .....use a periodical index.

Please answer the following questions on the answer sheet. Do not write on this form.

19. What did you <u>like</u> about the video tapes?

20. If you were the producer of the video tapes, and were planning to revise them, what changes would you make?

THE EFFECTIVE USE OF SLIDES IN BIBLIOGRAPHIC INSTRUCTION

Donna Bentley and Kathryn Moore
Walter Clinton Jackson Library
University of North Carolina at Greensboro

For several years, reference librarians at the University of North Carolina at Greensboro (UNCG) have used slide packages for bibliographic instruction (BI) in many subject areas. These slides are used during BI lectures to illustrate the procedures and sources used in a search strategy. A bibliography and other handouts usually accompany the slide lecture. While not as flashy as videotapes, slides have many advantages: they are instructionally adaptable, inexpensive to produce, and if well done, a very effective method of presenting information. Disadvantages exist as well: slides cannot be prepared at the last minute and mechanical failure must be anticipated. Slides with text can be difficult to read in large lecture halls. The use of microcomputer graphics programs to enhance the image, such as Pagemaker, can solve this problem.

Depending on campus photographic resources, slides can be easy and relatively inexpensive to produce. At UNCG, since BI is considered part of university instruction, the Learning Resources Center will produce slides at no charge to the library. Librarians should not attempt to produce slides themselves unless they are able to spend the time to do a professional job. Poorly done slides look amateurish. Professionally produced slides can be very appealing, especially if interspersed with amusing pictures to capture the attention of the audience.

The versatility of slides is an attractive advantage. Many slides can be used in more than one context. When new reference sources arrive, it is very easy to make a new slide and add it to the appropriate package. When lecturing, the librarian can interact with the class and combine viewing the slides with class discussion. Slide packages can also help new librarians teach unfamiliar subject areas.

THE LEARNING CYCLE: AN ALTERNATIVE TO THE LECTURE METHOD OF LIBRARY INSTRUCTION

Janet Sheets
Moody Memorial Library
Baylor University

A learning cycle adapted from Piagetian theory can provide one viable alternative to the lecture as a method of library instruction in many classes. A standard learning cycle has three phases: exploration, invention, and application. The exploration phase involves the student actively working on a problem with minimal guidance. During the invention phase, the instructor helps the students pull together what they have learned in phase one. This might include defining terms and explaining concepts or principles. The third phase, application, reinforces the learning and transfers it to a new situation.

In the summer of 1986, I attended a six-week teaching institute at Baylor University during which the learning cycle was taught. Each participant wrote a learning cycle and also critiqued those presented by colleagues. In the subsequent fall semester, I refined the cycle I had developed for the institute and used it in an "Introduction to Social Work" library instruction session. Since I had taught this class successfully for six previous semesters, I was somewhat surprised to find how much better I liked this new approach. Not only did the students react positively during the class hour, but the set of exercise sheets completed out of class showed more imagination and grasp of the material taught than in any previous semester.

During the LOEX instruction session, I will discuss the concept of a learning cycle and illustrate its use in the social work class. I will provide copies of the instructions to the students and the in-class worksheets as well as the take-home exercise sheets. I will cover suggestions for successful use of learning cycles and mention several pitfalls to avoid.

CONCRETE THOUGHT	FORMAL THOUGHT
(a) Needs reference to familiar actions, objects, and observable properties	Can reason with concepts, relationships, abstract properties, axioms, and theories; uses symbols to express ideas
(b) Uses classification, conservation, and seriation reasoning patterns in relation to concrete items (a) above. Has limited and intuitive understanding of formal reasoning patterns	Applies classification, conservation, seriation, combinatorial, proportional, probabilistic, correlational, and controlling variables reasoning in relation to abstract items (a) above
(c) Needs step-by-step instructions in a lengthy procedure	Can plan a lengthy procedure given certain overall goals and resources
(d) Is not aware of his own reasoning, inconsistencies among various statements he makes, or contradictions with other known facts	Is aware and critical of his own reasoning, actively seeks checks on the validity of his conclusions by appealing to other known information

LEARNING CYCLE

EXPLORATION

Introduces students to new material
and ideas. Gives them the opportunities
to work with objects and make observations.
Allows them to ask their own questions and
follow their own interest.

INVENTION

Introduces or explains concepts or
principles. Formal vocabulary may
be presented.

APPLICATION

Concepts explored in the first two stages
are used and applied in an assignment.
Reinforces a concept and aids transference
of a concept to a new situation.

FEATURES OF AN EFFECTIVE LEARNING CYCLE

1. Developmental listening

2. Use of the concrete

3. Sequencing

4. Collaboration

5. Perspective taking

6. Inquiry structuring

TWO EXAMPLES OF LEARNING CYCLES

	Data Processing Class	Human Values Class
EXPLORATION	Students work in small groups to verbalize and record in writing the steps followed in washing a car.	Students introduce themselves to each other including something they want the others to know about themselves. Comments are recorded on cards and given to small groups, whose task is to cluster them on the basis of their similarities.
INVENTION	Students are introduced to flow-charting convention and asked to generate, as a class, a description of car-washing using this format.	Students share their classification systems and, as a class, discuss similarities among the systems. They are then asked to decide whether what they had been doing had anything to do with human values. They realize that not only did their statement reveal valuing but also their systems did.
APPLICATION	Students work on their own or in small groups to generate a description of another common process with which they are familiar, and go on to produce a flowchart of that process.	Values students collect cases illustrating "valuing" in their environment.

LEARNING CYCLE   4MAT
―――――――――――   ――――

Exploration   Concrete experience

                                        Reflective experience

Invention   Abstract Conceptualization

Application   Active Experimentation

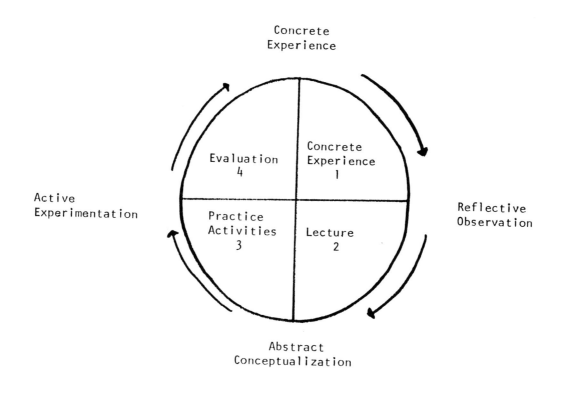

SOCIAL WORK 2305

BIBLIOGRAPHIC INSTRUCTION

Goal of Instruction: To learn how to use and how to find some library sources which
                         will help social workers as they practice their profession.

In class project: We will divide into small groups of about 4 students. Each group
                         will be given four sources from among the following types of
                         library sources:

        (1) Book
        (2) Volume of a specialized encyclopedia
        (3) Volume of a periodical index
        (4) Issue of a journal
        (5) Government publication
        (6) Directory

Each group should use the worksheets supplied and accomplish the following:

A. Identify one specific way each source could be used by a social worker. Briefly
    describe the professional situation and list the specific way the source could
    be used.

    An example of a possible response would be:

        SOURCE: Social Work Research and Abstracts

        A SOCIAL WORKER WHO --- has been assigned to work with battered women
        and wants to make sure of current research

        COULD USE THIS SOURCE TO --- find up-to-date review articles in professional
        journals

        AN EXAMPLE IS ON PAGE 82

B. Think about this book or periodical and about possible ways you could have used
    to find it in Moody Library. Be imaginative and list as many ways as you can
    think of. Guesses are allowed!

C. After discussion, put a star by the ways most likely to find you the source
    most quickly.

SOCIAL WORK 2305

BIBLIOGRAPHIC INSTRUCTION
WORKSHEET

SOURCE:

A. A SOCIAL WORKER WHO ------

    COULD USE THIS SOURCE TO ------

    AN EXAMPLE IS ON PAGE _____

B. Think about this book or periodical and about possible ways you could have used to
    find it in Moody Library. Be imaginative and list as many ways as you can think
    of. Guesses are allowed!

C. After our discussion, go back through the ways you listed in B above and star those
    which you feel are the most likely to find you the reference book the most quickly.

The Learning Cycle: an alternative to the lecture
method of library instruction

LOEX Library Instruction Conference - May 7 & 8, 1987

I. BACKGROUND/THEORY

Ault, Kay. "Improving College Teaching through Adapting Learning Styles Theory into Practice." Midwest Regional Conference on English in the Two-Year College. St. Louis, MO: 13-15 February 1986. ERIC ED 272 494.

Jackson, M.W. and M.T. Prosser. "De-lecturing. A Case Study of the Implementation of Small Group Teaching." Higher Education 14 (1985) 651-663.

McCarthy, Bernice. The 4MAT System: Teaching to Learning Styles with Right/Left Mode Techniques. Oak Brook, ILL: Excel Inc., 1980.

Mevarech, Zemira R. and Shulamit Werner. "Are Mastery Learning Strategies Beneficial for Developing Problem Solving Skills?" Higher Education 14 (1985) 425-432.

Meyers, Chet. Teaching Students to Think Critically. San Francisco: Jossey-Bass Publishers, 1986.

Shuell, Thomas J. "Cognitive Conceptions of Learning." Review of Educational Research. 56.4 (1986): 411-36.

Williams, Connie K. and Constance Kamii. "How Do Children Learn by Handling Objects?" Young Children 42.1 (1986): 23-26.

II. LIBRARY INSTRUCTION

Aluri, Rao. "Application of Learning Theories to Library-Use Instruction." Libri 31 (August 1981): 140-152.

Aluri, Rao and Mary Reichel. "Learning Theories and Bibliographic Instruction." Bibliographic Instruction and the Learning Process: Theory, Style and Motivation. Ed. Carolyn A. Kirkendall. Ann Arbor, MI: Pierian Press, 1984.

Oberman-Soroka Cerise. "Petals Around a Rose: Abstract Reasoning and Bibliographic Instruction." Association of College and Research Libraries, ALA Convention. New York, 1 July, 1980. ERIC ED 229 013.

III. BIBLIOGRAPHIES

Johnson, Judy. "Application of Learning Theory to Bibliographic Instruction: An Annotated Bibliography." Research Strategies (1986) 138-141.

Discussion Group Handouts
and Sample Materials from
the LOEX Clearinghouse
Collection

TIPS FOR *Better* LIBRARY ASSIGNMENTS

Library assignments and projects can provide students with valuable learning experiences if there is adequate advance planning and there are clear objectives. Without these prerequisites, the assignments can be frustrating for all concerned.

COMMON ASSIGNMENT PROBLEMS

1. ### The Mob Scene

   An entire class comes to the library to find one book or article. What happens?

   Mayhem! Catalogs are toppled and index volumes are torn apart. The first student to find the material rips out the pages, hides the book, or shares only with his friends.

   Solution: Create individual or small-group assignments on a variety of topics requiring students to use different reference tools.

2. ### The Shot-in-the-Dark Assignment

   An incomplete or incorrect citation is thrown out to students. What happens?

   Murder! Students and librarians struggle for hours trying to find the material.

   Solution: Verify references. Make sure the library owns the cited material. Give students clear, complete instructions--preferably in writing. Define any discipline-related terms students do not know and librarians might not recognize.

3. ### The Scavenger Hunt

   Students are asked to find obscure bits of information. What happens?

   Chaos! Pulling every book off the shelf is not considered an efficient research strategy.

   Solution: Instruction in research methodology. Show students samples of library research strategies for different disciplines. Develop meaningful library assignments which also teach critical thinking.

Arizona State University

LIBRARY
& LEARNING RESOURCES
CALIFORNIA STATE UNIVERSITY
L O N G   B E A C H

Search Strategy Outline

Information Guide

1. Select a topic for research:_____

2. Read an encyclopedia article, or your textbook to:
    a. obtain an overview of the topic
    b. identify and list potential search terms
    c. note significant references or citations in the bibliography

    Encyclopedia or textbook:_____
    Topic(s) looked up:_____
    Possible subject terms to use:_____
    Books to consider using (author & title):_____

3. Narrow your topic:
    a. decide which aspect of your topic to investigate
    b. limit the topic by geography, scope, time, individuals affected, etc.

    Narrowed topic:_____

4. Revise your list of search terms (2.b.) and authors/titles (2.c.) for your
    narrower topic:_____

5. Search the card catalog for books:
    a. translate search terms into <u>Library</u> <u>of</u> <u>Congress</u> <u>Subject</u> <u>Headings</u> (<u>LCSH</u>)
        terms.

    Useful <u>LCSH</u> headings and subdivisions:_____
    Other possible <u>LCSH</u> headings:_____

    b. call numbers of books you found in Step 2.c.:_____

    c. additional subject tracings from the catalog cards of items identified above:
        _____

6. Search appropriate periodical and newspaper indexes:

Index:_____
    Dates searched:_____
    Subject headings used:_____

7. Locate periodicals and newspapers by using the Serials Record:

    Journal title, volume, date:_____
    Call number:_____ Format: Bound Microfilm Unbound

    Journal title, volume, date:_____
    Call number:_____ Format: Bound Microfilm Unbound

8. Initiate Inter-Library Loan requests for material <u>not</u> owned by Library.

California State University, Long Beach

9. For statistics, consult the card catalog and periodical indexes (5.a., 6.), using the subdivision `--Statistics.' Also use the <u>American Statistics Index</u>:
    _____

10. For federal government documents, use the <u>Monthly Catalog of U.S. Government Publications</u> for Superintendent of Documents (SuDoc) numbers: _____

11. Consult with librarians in Reference Center (2W) to locate other sources of information, e.g., bibliograpies, directories, maps, graphs, audio-visual matericals, etc.

    Other sources:_____ _____ _____

12. Read and evaluate materials retrieved

13. Outline paper

14. First draft of paper

15. Revise and rewrite paper

16. Final draft of paper

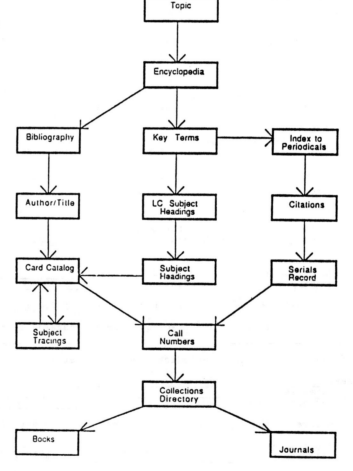

LKS & JT: 4/87 (Rev.)

LOEX 1987

Joan Ormondroyd
"In-House Training of Instruction Librarians"

QUESTIONS FOR DISCUSSION

1. What are the qualities needed for good teaching?

2. Should one use different methods of teaching with foreign students than with native speakers?

3. What advantages are there in video taping during a workshop? Are there any disadvantages?

4. What can we do to assure that any new staff we hire in our department will fit well into our instruction program?

5. Our director says her funds are severely limited. Are there ways to fund a workshop if we really go all out and have a great one?

6. Is there some way we can assure some form of on-going teacher training once the workshop is over -- or if we can't afford a workshop at all?

7. Should we really be providing in-house training? Shouldn't library schools take on that responsibility and make sure librarians are fully trained before they come into the profession?

8. Do librarians who prove to be poor teachers, or who refuse to take part in the instruction component of public services, really have a role in libraries today?

Cornell University

LAUNCHING YOUR COLLEGE ASSIGNMENT....

(with a minimum of hot air)

STEPS TO FOLLOW:		SOME HINTS:
1. Topic Selection:	Scan the course syllabus and other materials and find a topical area which is of major importance in the course. Assess the amount of material readily available (i.e. in the library). If material is available on a number of topics choose the one that most interests you.	Be sure you know what is meant by term paper, presentation, seminar, etc. (see DEFINITIONS on last page).
2. Defining your Topic:	Look over all the materials assigned for your course and read what you think might be relevant to your topic. Attempt to frame a title to your term paper and acquaint your instructor with your choice. If necessary get your instructor's opinion or ideas on your topic choice.	
3. The Safety Exit:	The last chance to leave the topic for another one. If up to this point you do not think there will be enough material available, or you do not think you have a clearly defined topic, pick another topic and begin again. You should have used up only a few of your precious study hours.	
4. Library Research:	Using the attached guide, advance through the various levels of research, if necessary using the librarians who will be at the reference/information desk. Remember to relate the amount of material you obtain to the size of your essay and the time you have available to do the project.	See outline of RESEARCH LEVELS.
5. Establishing a Point to "Take Off" From:	There are a number of ways to begin a term paper, but all begin with a statement of purpose, which is a statement of the topic you plan to explore (in detail). Keep this topic statement close at hand while doing your essay organization.	You might like to investigate "Study Skills for College" given by Student Services. Centre.
6. Establishing Some Type of Organization:	You can make or break your essay with organization. You should establish some system; if you have none, a card system might help. Do not attempt to read all your material; try rather to skim material and pick out what will be of value.	"Skills for College Library Research" examines how to organize as well as collect information.
7. Putting It All Together:	Once you have begun researching the topic, you might find that you have more information than you need. With your statement of purpose in mind, establish the importance of each idea, and the way in which it relates to the other ideas. Again, having each "unit" of information on a card helps.	See above. Douglas College's **Composition and Style Handbook**, produced by the English and Communications Department, is available at the bookstore or the library and will also give you some ideas.

Douglas College

8. Writing the
   Paper
   Twice (if
   possible):

Since this is what the instructor will mark it pays to produce a good paper. Hopefully you will leave yourself time to do one revision, but if not, remember the following points:

(1) Concentrate on the English, particularly noting that each paragraph has a topic sentence, and that paragraphs follow logically.

(2) If you are going to use quotations, either indirectly or directly, be sure you are aware of the way to quote and the system your instructor prefers (there is more than one).

(3) The most difficult parts of an essay, to most, are the introduction and the conconclusion. Concentrate on making these areas particularly effective.

(4) A paper that is neat, well presented, and on time can't hurt your ''cause''. It takes a little care and organization to guarantee a satisfactory presentation.

See the following information on PARAGRAPHS.

9. The Marks:

We sincerely hope you get a good grade, and trust this handout will help. If we can help in any other way let us know.

— The Library Staff

PARAGRAPHS

— A written assignment has an outline structure, and paragraphs fill out that structure.

— When rewriting the paper make sure that:
   (1) each paragraph has a reason to exist and has a topic sentence which makes the major point.
   (2) paragraphs have some link between them, and that new ideas are not introduced in a random manner.

— The first paragraph (the one that introduces the theme, the topic or the argument) is particularly important, so give it special attention.

— By the same token the final paragraph deserves more of your time. It can summarize, evaluate, and draw some conclusions.

Douglas College

LEVELS OF RESEARCH FOR ASSIGNMENTS

Level 1: Definition

— To know every term you are using in your thesis or statement of purpose is essential. Use whomever (your instructor) or whatever (a dictionary) to clarify what it is you are attempting to do.

— Quite often a subject dictionary (e.g. **Dictionary of Social Sciences**) is helpful.

Level 2: Overview

— Once you are sure what questions are to be answered, obtaining an overview (a general idea of the topic) can be a real help in understanding the broad areas of importance.

— Such works as encyclopedias, texts, collected essays, or surveys can help.

Level 3: Book Material

— Your major source. You don't necessarily need a great number of books, just books that are about your **particular** topic.

— The ability to find suitable book material is in direct relation to how well you can identify the subject headings used to categorize books — it's not always easy to find the right heading, so ask.

Level 4: Periodicals, Magazines, Journals

— These sources are great; short, concise, and up to date. **However, you must be able to use periodical indexes.** Frequently, articles are written as the result of specific research; thus a good deal of background knowledge can be required. Be sure you are ready to use the materials by having progressed through the various levels outlined.

Level 5: Special Materials

— There is a whole host of special reference works: maps, atlases, pamphlets, newspapers, and audio-visual materials that can be used at any level, depending on the complexity of the subject. Local subjects, current topics, law, and geography are just a few subjects that may require special materials.

Douglas College

SOME DEFINITIONS

Term Paper
Research Paper
Term Essay

All these terms are used by instructors to describe a paper that requires the student to do independent work with a variety of sources. Such papers usually involve footnotes, references, and bibliographies.

Report: objective
Review: subjective

A report usually means a short work on a reasonably limited topic (i.e. book report). Some instructors make the distinction between subjective reviews that require some research, and objective reports which simply recount a series of facts. Footnotes, references and bibliographies are not commonly part of report writing.

Presentation

Presentations most commonly are verbal reports given by one or more students. Presentations are short, and require no supporting paper.

Seminar

A seminar is an extended presentation which usually presumes a paper will be submitted upon which the seminar is based. Seminars are longer than presentations, and require considerable independent work, where footnotes, references, and bibliographies can be used.

Assignment

Any required piece of work, asked for by instructors, in which students are expected to do independent work.

Group Discussion

As the term implies, a topic discussed by a group of students. Frequently, the result of such discussion is the group being required to make a presentation.

Debate

A debate involves two groups of students adopting opposing sides of a stated controversy or argument. Debates can require considerable research but rarely require follow-up papers or notation.

N.B. Take care to check with your instructor which of the above definitions is applied to the particular assignments you do. Terms applied by instructors can vary greatly.

Douglas College

INDIANA UNIVERSITY AT SOUTH BEND LIBRARY

STUDENT FEEDBACK SHEET

Librarian's Name_____   Date_____

                                             Course Title_____
                                             _____

Please help us by taking a few moments to complete this form. All comments
are welcome.

        Rate each statement according to the degree that best describes how
        you feel: 1 = strongly agree   4 = disagree
                    2 = agree   5 = strongly disagree
                    3 = neutral

                                                     Agree   Disagree

1. In terms of what I think I will need for this course,   1 2 3 4 5
    the library instruction was valuable.

2. The handouts are clear and understandable.   1 2 3 4 5

3. I think that the handouts will be useful to me
    when I do library research.   1 2 3 4 5

4. Before this library instruction, I knew little
    about the library sources discussed today.   1 2 3 4 5

5. I found the taped tour of the IUSB Library helpful.   1 2 3 4 5

6. The Librarian used terms that I could understand.   1 2 3 4 5

7. The Librarian was well organized in the presentation. 1 2 3 4 5

8. The Librarian explained the material well.   1 2 3 4 5

9. The Librarian used examples and illustrations well.   1 2 3 4 5

10. The Librarian was audible and spoke clearly.   1 2 3 4 5

11. I felt free to ask questions during the session.   1 2 3 4 5

12. The encyclopedia is often the best place to begin
    looking for information on my topic.   True   False

13. Using the Library of Congress Subject Headings List
    will help me find the best subject heading to use when
    looking in the card catalog for books on my subject.   True   False

14. Using an index such as Readers' Guide (or something
    similar) will help me find journal articles about my
    topic.   True   False

Indiana University At South Bend

15. The amount of material presented was   ___ too little.
   ___ about right.
   ___ too much.

16. Which items discussed did you find the most useful?

   ___ background information   ___ indexes (i.e. Readers' Guide)
   ___ subject headings   ___ computer searching
   ___ card catalog   ___ interlibrary loan
   ___ reference sources   ___ other (please specify)

   _____
   _____

17. How many years have you attended IUSB?

   ___ less than one   ___ two
   ___ one   ___ three or more

Please feel free to write any other comments concerning this library instruction session.

Remember that the Library Staff is available to help you. You may stop at the Reference Desk or call us at 237-4440.

Indiana University At South Bend

STUDENT LIBRARY INSTRUCTION MANUAL

STUDENT EVALUATION

On a scale from 1 to 5, 1 being "not at all," 3 being "sort of" and 5 being "very much," indicate the one which reflects your feelings.

		Not at all		Sort of		Very Much
1. Was the instruction given in the Manual easy to understand?	1	2	3	4	5
2. Were the review questions helpful? (Do not answer if you did not do the reviews.)	1	2	3	4	5
3. Were the assignments helpful and appropriate?	1	2	3	4	5
4. Was it important to you to have your graded assignments returned before you took the exams?	1	2	3	4	5
5. Do you think the information and skills you acquired will be useful in the future?	1	2	3	4	5
6. Are you now able to use the card catalog with ease?	1	2	3	4	5
7. Are you now able to locate books in the library?	1	2	3	4	5
8. Are you now able to use the periodical indexes with ease?	1	2	3	4	5
9. Are you now able to locate periodicals in the library?	1	2	3	4	5
10. Are you now aware of different types of reference materials in the library?	1	2	3	4	5
11. Would you now be able to research a topic in the library?	1	2	3	4	5
12. Did the units and assignments prepare you for the examinations?	1	2	3	4	5

13. If you answered 1 or 2 for any of the above questions, please state why.

_____

_____

(Continued on other side)

Miami-Dade Community College Library

14. List the good points of Unit I. (Card Catalog and Reference Books)

_____

_____

_____

15. List the bad points of Unit I.

_____

_____

_____

16. List the good points of Unit II. (Periodicals)

_____

_____

_____

17. List the bad points of Unit II.

_____

_____

_____

Miami-Dade Community College Library

ASSESSING INFORMATION FOR A RESEARCH ASSIGNMENT
Eugene L. Freel Library
NORTH ADAMS STATE COLLEGE

TONE
- **Popular** information is created for the general public rather than specialists or experts.
- **Scholarly** information is produced by and for persons who are experts or specialists in a particular field of knowledge, and usually includes citations of other experts.

A periodical which contains popular information is usually called a **magazine**. *One which contains scholarly information is termed a* **journal**.

AUTHORITY
- What are the educational or professional credentials of the **author**?
- What is the reputation of the **publisher**?
- Does the author or publisher have a **bias** which might cause the information to be incomplete or misleading?

DISCIPLINARY PERSPECTIVE
- Is the information produced or considered valid by practitioners of your course's discipline?

RELATIVE AGE
- **Contemporary** information was created a relatively short time after the occurrence of the "event" which the information is about.
- **Retrospective** information was created a relatively long time after the "event" occurred.

An "event," as the term is used here, could be just about anything--a battle, the publication of a book, the life of a famous person, the flourishing of a philosophy or school of thought, a scientific discovery, etc.

SCOPE
- **Background** information (typically found in encyclopedias and other reference works) familiarizes you with a broad subject.
- **In-depth** information (found in most journal articles and circulating books) provides more thorough examination of a narrower topic.
- **Single fact** information (found in dictionaries, almanacs, and other reference works) consists of specific data (dates, definitions, etc.).

North Adams State College, Eugene L. Freel Library

LOEX 1987
David Johnson, Mary P. Key, Victoria Welborn
"Teaming Up with Classroom Faculty"

DISCUSSION QUESTIONS FOR LOEX 1987

1. Can there be true team-teaching where librarians are equal partners with instructors in course-related instruction without University administration endorsement.

2. Are the benefits, both tangible and intangible, of team-teaching worth the cost in terms of library personnel time to the reference librarian? to the user education librarian? to the library administrator?

3. Are exercises which for and/or strongly encourage the use of the search strategy good assignments.

4. Should exercise concerning specific tools be used.

5. How can librarians effectively evaluate their part of team-teaching. What follow up methods can be used.

Ohio State University

GIVE 'EM H!

Have you discovered certain techniques of instruction that have been particularly successful with students--especially undergraduates--in helping them to understand aspects of the library?

Share some of your **HINTS** *for explaining certain resources, processes, etc.*

What have you used as **HOOKS** *or attention-grabbers at the beginning of a session?*

Give some examples of **HUMOR** *that have gone over well, that have added to (rather than detracted from) the presentation.*

. Write or type those items on the back of this sheet. Send, either signed or anonymously, to Cynthia Wright Swaine by Friday, September 26, to have them included in an informal compilation that could help all of us.*

*Other hints you may have to share may be forwarded to the Library Instruction Librarian at any time.

Old Dominion University

Part II:
Response

Here are the responses received for our first on-paper sharing of teaching tips for library instruction. If you have others to share, send them to Cynthia. Thank you.

HOOKS

- I try to challenge them to stay awake for the duration of the class. (Trade secret as to what I say to them.)

- Get the group's attention with a "hearty" greeting. If there is no response initially, do it again until there is a response. Usually the second time, a response is given.

- A brief self-introduction including your credentials and qualifications helps to legitimize you as a teacher.

- I put a series of numbers on the chalkboard in advance. The series looks something like this:

        303-48-6759
        804-440-4178
        10017
        GWV 924
        QA 76 .B3
        22Q4301

I get the students involved by getting them to tell me which number is a license plate, a phone number, etc., leaving the LC call number and InfoTrac reference number until the end. We briefly acknowledge how there are so many numbers, it can get confusing, but how we <u>do</u> get to recognize numerical formats. We get into LC classification at this point.

Old Dominion University

- Sometimes, if the class is long enough, I will put a slip of paper on each desk and ask students at the very beginning to write down the <u>one thing</u> they most want to know about how to use the library. They turn them in anonymously. Then I see what their problems are and can treat those with special emphasis.

HUMOR

- Comedienne/Librarian/Teacher is an unlikely combination but it is important to try to keep it light. I try to joke about how dull and boring it all is.

- I explain LCSH by supposing one of the students wants to write a paper on bubble gum. If she can't find it in the COMCAT (the subject heading, not the sticky stuff), she might just give up and go home. Instead LCSH can tell what the correct heading is; it might be CHEWING GUM or GUM or CANDY AND GUM.

HINTS

- I don't know if I am successful or not, but I always have this strange feeling that students don't understand why there are so many indexes. Also, they don't understand why we don't have everything that is indexed in the indexes. To help them grasp the problem, I like to play a guessing game of (1) how many journals are published in the world, and (2) how many of these does this library get?

- Ask two or three students at random to explain the assignment. You'll get a variety of answers. This can help to reinforce the point of "knowing the purpose of the research to be attempted."

- Distribute handouts in advance face down and ask that they not look at them until requested. I find students otherwise trying to read the handouts as I'm speaking if I don't do this. It saves time to distribute them in advance.

- After reviewing a type of material, break for questions and answers about that type, for example, indexes. Ask 2 students to look briefly at one index and find a citation under a subject related to the project. I usually choose 2 that perhaps were not as attentive as I think they should have been. This puts the others on alert! It is done in a non-embarassing and non-threatening manner.

- Assure them that you and your colleagues will help to the best of your and our ability and that they should not hesitate to ask for assistance.

- Reinforce the need for accurate note taking. Write complete citations so that time is not wasted re-checking because, for example, the page number was not noted.

Old Dominion University

Involve the students by asking questions instead of doing so much talking at them.

I often relate my own confusion or ineptitude in the past when I've gone into a new library. I say that all libraries are different (and get a lot of nods and knowing looks) but they have a lot in common (e.g., some type of catalog that lists major holdings). They relate to me better when they realize I'm human, that I, too, realize libraries can be confusing.

A former ODU librarian related an experience with using the yellow pages to find women's clothing stores. She looked under CLOTHING (no luck) and DRESSES (no luck). Finally she used the index and found the proper term: WOMEN'S APPAREL. She compares this experience to using LCSH before the COMCAT subject section.

For the young, inexperienced, possibly unmotivated students, I try to relate the need for knowing about the library to their own personal interests (drugs? sex? rock music? etc.) beyond the college curriculum. I tell them this library is full of information on many topics, but to get to it all, one has to have the "key" (i.e., know how to use the catalogs, indexes, etc.).

WARNING: The printing of the above suggestions submitted by ODU librarians does not necessarily constitute approval or guaranteed success by the Library Instruction Librarian! cws

Old Dominion University

Evaluating for Teaching Effectiveness

Discussion Questions

1. Professor Smerdley has just come to talk to you about a library session for his sophomore-level introductory course in meteorology. His students will be required to write a 3-5 page paper using professional scholarly journals. He feels that a 20-minute session will be adequate, and that Science Citation Index is the most important tool to cover. Further, several students have told him that they have already had the library class in freshman English, so he questions as to whether they need to be there. What kind(s) of evaluative instrument(s) could you use to make this class session more productive? To make future sessions with Smerdley's classes better?

2. As Coordinator of Library Instruction, you are responsible for the training and evaluation of librarians whose duties include instruction. Margie Newcomer, a recent library graduate, has just been hired to serve as a reference/instruction librarian. At her interview, she expressed interest and enthusiasm in teaching. However, now that she's on the job, it's obvious that she is very nervous about her lack of experience. What kind of evaluation tools or procedures can you design to help her grow in confidence and expertise? Would you use the same ones to assess her performance for the personnel committee? Why or why not?

3. For the past 5 years, you have been teaching a 2-hour session every semester to introductory psychology research class. It is almost unbearable to think of going in and talking about Psychological Abstracts one more time, but you must. What kinds of evaluative techniques might you use to renew your enthusiasm?

4. Your library director has just called a meeting of all the department heads to announce that the library will have a 20% budget cut for the next fiscal year. It is now too late to put into place any kind of evaluation system. What should you have done in order to be in a position to defend your program?

5. Your tenure decision will be made a year and a half from now. Like other faculty members on campus, you are expected to prepare a dossier which demonstrates your competencies in teaching, research, and service. What kinds of evidence can evaluative techniques provide you? What tools can you use to gather this evidence in order to make the strongest possible case for yourself?

Philadelphia College of Pharmacy and Science

BIBLIOGRAPHIC INSTRUCTION EVALUATION FORM

Please take a few minutes to fill out this form. Be as open as possible with your responses. Remember! It is with your cooperation that Bibliographic Instruction can become a most effective library service. Please fill out both sides of form. THANK YOU.

RETURN TO: Joan D'Andrea, BI Coordinator, Library Room 304

FROM: DATE: TIME: COURSE NUMBER:

WORKSHOP ASSESSMENT

1. What were your objectives in scheduling this class?

2. To what extent were these objectives met?

3. Please list for our information those aspects of the class you felt were most helpful.

4. What aspects did you feel were superfluous? Why?

5. How would you suggest that the class might have been improved?

6. Would you consider scheduling a workshop in future semesters?

7. Would you recommend a bibliographic instruction session to your colleagues?

St. John's University

INSTRUCTOR PERFORMANCE EVALUATION

A.A. = ABOVE AVERAGE   A. = AVERAGE   B.A. = BELOW AVERAGE

OVERALL RATING: Poor 1 2 3 4 5 Excellent

	B.A.	A.	A.A.
PERSONAL IMPACT:			
Appearance	___	___	___
Self-confidence and poise	___	___	___
Voice tone and mannerisms	___	___	___
Attitude toward class (friendly, bored, etc.)	___	___	___
DELIVERY EFFECTIVENESS:			
General knowledge of subject	___	___	___
Ability to present information clearly	___	___	___
Well-organized in presentation	___	___	___
Ability to communicate with minimum reliance on notes	___	___	___
Avoidance of irrelevant details	___	___	___
Ability to use examples clearly	___	___	___
Ability to encourage interest and to stimulate discussion from group	___	___	___
Ability to answer questions clearly and concisely	___	___	___

PLEASE LIST ANY OTHER ADDITIONAL COMMENTS OR SUGGESTIONS.

St. John's University

Southern Methodist University
Fondren Library
Reference Department

Survey of English 1302 students,
Spring 1987
Rhetoric Instructor_____

Please help us evaluate and improve the library instruction session in the Rhetoric curriculum. Complete and return this questionnaire to your Rhetoric instructor as soon as possible. Thank you for your help.

1) Did you attend the library instruction session with your Rhetoric class? **yes   no**

2) Did you find the library instruction helpful for your Rhetoric assignment? **yes   no**

3) Based on your experience, would you like the library instruction to spend more, less, or about the same amount of time on the following topics?

card catalog	**more**	**less**	**about the same**
finding books	**more**	**less**	**about the same**
using periodical indexes	**more**	**less**	**about the same**
finding periodicals	**more**	**less**	**about the same**
using newspaper indexes	**more**	**less**	**about the same**
finding newspapers	**more**	**less**	**about the same**
using and finding microforms	**more**	**less**	**about the same**
finding background information	**more**	**less**	**about the same**

any other topic?_____

4) Did you use the library guide "Introduction to Library Research" prepared by the librarians? **yes   no**   Was it helpful? **yes   no**

5) Was a walking tour an appropriate format for this instruction?   **yes   no**

If not, what type of instruction would you find most helpful?
a) classroom lecture given by a librarian
b) self-guided tour or instruction with library providing variety of instructional handouts
c) other_____

6) Did the librarian explain things clearly?   **yes   no   somewhat**

7) Did the librarian seem knowledgeable about your assignment?
yes   no   somewhat

8) Did the librarian seem interested and willing to help you?
yes   no   somewhat

Southern Methodist University

9) Do you think library instruction should continue as a part of the Rhetoric curriculum?

yes   no

10) If yes, which of the following options would you prefer?
   a) one class in the spring semester
   b) one class in the fall semester
   c) one class in both spring and fall semesters
   d) two classes in spring semester
   e) other_____

11) Do you think this instruction will help you in other courses? **yes   no   perhaps**

12) How often do you usually go to the library in a typical week?
   5-7 times   3-4   1-2   rarely

13) When you go to the library, do you go to:
   a) study?   **often   sometimes   rarely**
   b) read reserve materials?   **often   sometimes   rarely**
   c) do research for class assignments?   **often   sometimes   rarely**
   d) read or browse?   **often   sometimes   rarely**
   e) meet friends?   **often   sometimes   rarely**
   f) other? _____

14) How often have you asked questions at the Reference/Information desk?
   never   once   more than once

15) Did you get any help?   **yes   no   somewhat**

16) How did library instruction class affect your willingnes to ask for help at the
   Reference/Information desk?   **More willing to ask for help**
                                  Less willing to ask for help
                                  No change

17) Would you voluntarily participate in a library instruction program if it were not part
   of a class assignment?
   yes   no

18) Do you have any other comments about the library instruction or the library in
   general?

Southern Methodist University

Dear Colleague:

In order to improve the presentations given to library classes, Penfield librarians are interested in soliciting feedback from the faculty members who are involved in the sessions. We would appreciate your taking the time during the presentation to respond to the items below. The information you provide will go only to the librarian conducting the session for his or her use in improving presentations.

I.   CLARITY

How clearly was the information presented?

Was the information at the right level for your students (neither too elementary nor too complex)?

Did the librarian use appropriate examples to explain abstract ideas?

What needs to be clearer?

"We developed this form to give to faculty members. However, even though everyone thought it was a good idea, no one's used it. I guess it is pretty scary."

SUNY/Oswego, Penfield Library

Please note any concepts, jargon, or references that students might have trouble understanding. Each discipline uses its own jargon and concept shortcuts; we need to know when we've referred to ideas in ways which your students will have difficulty understanding.

II. RELATIONSHIP TO STUDENTS

Are there things about college students in general, or this class in particular, which would be helpful for the librarian to know about?

III. LOOKING AHEAD

What can be done to ensure a better presentation next time? (Examples: librarian's better understanding of the assignment, timing of the class during the semester, information or materials that the students need ahead of time.)

IV. Any other comments of use:

Thank you!

SUNY/Oswego, Penfield Library

GUIDELINES FOR CLASS OBSERVATION BY LIBRARIANS

1. Presentation Skills:

-has adequate vocal delivery (audible, varied in level and pitch, interesting)

-demonstrates energy and enthusiasm

-uses good body movement (appropriate gestures, avoids standing in one spot)

-uses good eye contact

-uses media appropriately: visuals can be seen, contribute to class understanding

2. Clarity of Presentation:

-avoids jargon

-uses examples to illustrate abstract ideas

-has logical organization

-relates to what students already know

3. Appropriateness of Content:

-is at right level for the individual class

-fits time frame well (covers neither too much nor too little)

-fits class assignment

-has accurate and sufficient information

SUNY/Oswego, Penfield Library

GUIDELINES FOR CLASS OBSERVATION BY LIBRARIANS

4. Generalization of Subject Matter:

   -allows for student practice of skills

   -uses examples which relate to other research situations which the student
    may encounter in the future

5. Relationship to Students:

   -shows understanding of students' problems

   -accepts and encourages student questions

6. Relationship with Instructor:

   -has obtained adequate knowledge of assignment

   -works with instructor during class

7. Reaction of Students:

   -uses methods to involve students

   -students seem interested

   -uses appropriate ways to give students hands-on experience

SUNY/Oswego, Penfield Library

GENERAL GUIDELINES FOR NON PRINT INSTRUCTION MATERIALS

Preparing non-print materials for library instruction requires careful thought and planning. This list offers a number of things to consider. Regardless of the type of media selected, keep the library's objectives and the patron's needs foremost in mind. Use local talent within the institution to help with both planning and production.

Beginning Considerations

-Study the media options
slides   video tapes/discs   combination of forms
tapes   transparencies
films   opaque projector
filmstrips   computer

-What equipment and space will be required?
recorders   tapes
screens   earphones
large room   carrels

-Cost to library and/or institution

-Operation and maintenance

-Revision possibilities

Script Considerations

-Keep it short, concise, clear & literate, avoiding library jargon
-Keep it light, funny but not cute
-Can it be updated and revised easily?
-Allow for spontaneous remarks when producing

Recording Considerations

-Use high quality equipment
-Use professional readers
-Use music carefully: it assists in the flow of text but can also distract
-Delivery should be slow and clear

Photography/Filming Considerations

-Look for action and interesting pictures
-Vary angles
-Fade in, fade out
-Film twice as much material as will be needed
-Watch the composition
-Avoid filming too much at once

SUNY/Syracuse, Moon Library

GENERAL GUIDELINES FOR PRINTED INSTRUCTION MATERIALS

When a library uses printed instruction materials, much thought and planning should be given to the use of the materials, design and production. This checklist presents a number of specific things to remember and consider. The three main aspects overlap and should be considered simultaneously. It is also helpful to develop a good working relationship with the print shop or other publication and design (graphics) professionals at your institution.

Use of the Material

    -have objectives for the materials
    -consider the audience (class, tour, handout)
    -will the material self instruct
    -will the material supplement other instruction (tour, class)

Design of the Material

    -text of the material (What will it say?)
    -text should be clear, concise and easy to understand (avoid
        library jargon); proof read carefully
    -use illustrations (drawings, charts, diagrams, maps,
        photographs, library logo)
    -plan a print style (lettering, transfer letters, typing,
        combination of styles)
    -plan spacing and attractive layout
    -paste up and proof read carefully
    -consider paper to use
        size, one sheet or more, folded, stapled, use both sides
        (can't be used for scrap), 3-hole punch (for notebooks),
        colors are nice
    -consider a standard format using library logo
    -use local talent (students, staff, graphics department)
        copy should be clear and neat
    -consider revision possibilities
    -include name of author/librarian, library and date
    -indicate copyright restrictions

Production considerations

    -cost to library and/or institution
    -in house and/or institution facilities
    -commercial printing
    -revision, costs and possibilities
    -size of type
    -style of type
    -color of paper and ink
    -weight of paper
    -reduction or enlargement possibilities
    -amount of material to duplicate
    -use local talent to help with duplicating ideas.

F. Franklin Moon Library, SUNY College of Environmental Science &
    Forestry, Syracuse, NY 13210

SUNY/Syracuse, Moon Library

USING AUDIO-VISUAL MATERIALS FOR INSTRUCTION: PROS AND CONS

Advantages

    Can reach a wide audience
    Do not need faculty approval
    Once prepared, saves constant repetition of core information
        and staff time
    Are available commercially
    Can make multiple copies for showing in different locations
    Excellent for setting a welcoming tone & friendly atmosphere
    Can combine orientation and instruction
    Sometimes are easily adaptable to settings
    If a tour, does not disrupt or disturb regular library routine
    Helpful to users who won't ask
    Requires little space to display
    Available when/ where needed
    Draws and holds users' attention
    Allows library tools to be seen clearly
    Meets multi-media expectations of the students and users
    Supplements orientation; instruction in other forms
    Excellent for point-of-use instruction
    Good PR mechanism

        Disadvantages

        Takes time, money & expertise to prepare & maintain
        Requires frequent updating
        Commercially-available programs not always appropriate
        Possible copyright problems
        Librarian-personal contact not available; impersonal
        Need outlets, lighting, equipment
        Special evaluation design necessary
        Must be of high quality to hold attention
        Users often turned off by a-v; intimidated
        User must be motivated to watch entire program
        Difficult to be detailed and concise
        Do not teach concepts or search strategy as a rule
        A-V not always effective in terms of retention

SUNY/Syracuse, Moon Library

SUGGESTED OUTLINE PLAN OF ACTION FOR BASIC LIBRARY
ORIENTATION/INSTRUCTION

To Establish a Program
    Consider the Academic Environment:
        -Define academic setting, considering: institutional nature,
            size, subject emphasis, programs, core courses, distribution
            requirement, resources
        -Profile student/library user population
        -Assess library personnel/materials
        -Discuss tentative ideas with administrators/faculty
        -Assess library interests/needs of total academic community
        -Determine initial target/pilot group and program format for
            maximum practicality/effectiveness
        -Discuss proposed program & organizational structure with
            entire staff/administrators: finalize plans
        -Contact the LOEX Clearinghouse for sample ideas to save time
            and avoid duplication of effort

    Plan the Library Instruction Program Details:
        -Write objectives for the program methods, utilizing
            faculty/staff input
        -Delineate personnel/support staff needs & responsibilities,
            needs for equipment/facilities/support services
        -List possible instructional materials to be prepared
        -Compose a tentative budget
        -Devise a projected timetable for program implementation
        -Design/plan evaluation methods/procedures

To Implement the Program
    Publicize the Program to:
        -Library staff members
        -Faculty
        -Students
        -All administrators

    Prepare Instructional Materials to Support Teaching Methods:
        -Printed guides, worksheets, evaluation forms, handouts, etc.
        -Media materials, if needed

    Test Program on Limited Portion of Population

    Implement Program Fully:
        -Solicit support/involve library staff members
        -Keep detailed statistics
        -Conduct some evaluation each term
        -Write/revise annual objectives to keep attainment possible
        -Continue to publicize the program
        -Read in the field/attend conferences for inspiration

    Remain Flexible and Patient:
        -Revise and refine -- simplify -- expand

    Keep the Program Working, changing as user needs change, for
        6-10 years.

SUNY/Syracuse, Moon Library

EDUCATION & PSYCHOLOGY LIBRARY
INSTRUCTION /ORIENTATION EVALUATION FORM

Name (optional)_____

Course Department and Number_____

Course Title_____

Name and Title of Course Instructor_____

Class (check One)   Fr____ So____ Jr____ Sr_____ Master's____ Doctoral____

Number of Quarters at UCLA_____
* *
Please circle your response to the following questions.

1. Have you used the Education & Psychology Library before?   yes   no

2. Have you used other UCLA Libraries before?   yes   no

3. If yes on #2, which one(s) did you use?_____

4. Was the librarian's presentation clear?   yes   no

5. Was there enough opportunity to ask questions?   yes   no

6. Were your questions answered to your satisfaction?   yes   no

7. Did you learn anything new about the following:

        a. _____   yes   no

        b. _____   yes   no

        c. _____   yes   no

        d. _____   yes   no

        e. _____   yes   no

        f. _____   yes   no

8. On the whole did you find the presentation useful?   yes   no

9. Would you be interested in additional instruction?   yes   no

    If yes, what topics would you like covered?

University of California, Los Angeles

LOEX 1987

Keith Cottam
"Teaching: No Greater Professional Role"

Questions for Discussion

1. What is the significance of the difference between <u>what</u> is taught and
    <u>how</u> it is taught, and how do you apply the <u>difference</u> in your own teaching?

2. You are considered an authority in the field of librarianship and you
    work to enhance your expertise, but how do you also work to improve
    your skills and techniques as a teacher?

3. What constitutes effective teaching?

4. What do you do as a teacher to cause your students to learn?

5. How do you personally evaluate the effectiveness of your teaching?

6. How do you get yourself intellectually involved in the business and challenge
    of teaching?

7. Does research, either into the discipline of librarianship or into the
    teaching process, lead to better teaching?

8. How do you facilitate interaction -- continuing interaction -- between
    yourself and the students you teach in the classroom after the students
    have left the classroom?

9. How do you effect breakthroughs, progress and enhancements in your
    teaching abilities?

10. What is your attitude about the place of your professional degree --
    the MLS -- in your role as teacher?

University of Wyoming

RULES FOR GOOD TEACHING

Develop a simple conversational style
    Remember that you are talking to other human beings
    Talk as you would to one person
    Look at and interact with the audience; make eye contact

Voice
    Let it out
    Start slowly & gradually increase to your natural rate of speaking
    Articulate clearly; practice volume control; use a lower pitch - to
        reach a large audience without giving the impression of shouting

Poise, posture & gesture
    Stand in a comfortable position
    Use a podium if it makes you feel at ease
    Avoid pacing back & forth, but do not give the impression of a
        statue; as a general rule, it is better not to sit down
    Use gestures freely & easily; avoid overuse

Put yourself into your teaching
    Be courteous & show good taste
    Never talk down to an audience, but make no assumptions about what
        they should know
    Speak with confidence but not cockiness; be authoritative
    Be prepared; know your subject well
    Be sure your materials are well organized & that your ideas are fully
        developed
    Make your transitions clear
    Include a summary of the main points in your conclusion

Welcome questions
    Encourage questions by being available & open to your audience
    Make sure that everyone can hear the question & the answer; repeat
        the question if necessary
    You can often turn the question back to other students for their
        reactions. The teacher should not be the source of all knowledge.
    Be flexible. If a question is worthwhile and the class shows a great
        deal of interest, expand the topic but make arrangements to get
        back to the planned subject matter
    Last but not least, don't be afraid to admit you don't know the
        answer

Listen to your audience
    Concentrate on what is being said
    Don't interrupt- give the student time to say what he/she has to say
    Listen for what is not said, for the real question
    Be patient. It may all seem very obvious to you, but remember what a
        complicated maze a library really is to an outsider.

Selecting visual aids
    Choose a visual aid appropriate to your room arrangement (slides are
        hard to see in a room without curtains)
    Be sure the visual aid is:
        large enough to be seen by all
        simple and easy to understand
        neat & attractive - as professional looking as possible

    Joan Ormondroyd, Cornell University; notes from a 1979 presentation

Cornell University

LECTURE EFFECTIVENESS CHECKLIST/OUTLINE

Physical Appearance

    Good eye contact
    Distracting nervous gestures
    Movement during lecture
    Friendly

Voice

    Consistently clear
    Consistently audible
    Variety
    Stress important points

Objectives

    Clear what class is to learn from outset
    Objectives used throughout lecture
    Objectives stressed in review

Intended level

    Was class level established?
    Too difficult
    Too elementary

Content

    Organization of content clear-lecture moves in logical fashion
    Relevant to objectives
    Clear, interesting examples
    Enough variety to maintain interest
    Location of materials given

Class Participation

    Ask questions
    Questions clear to listeners
    Leave plenty of time for answers
    Questions aid in developing a point

Audio-visuals and Blackboard Use

    Easy to see
    Used effectively
    Develop or stress a point

Review

    Used throughout lecture to stress all major ideas
    No unnecessary details discussed
    More than one method used

Notes for librarians from Winthrop College, Rock Hill SC 1981

Winthrop College

Bibliographies

BIBLIOGRAPHIC INSTRUCTION: RECOMMENDED READING

Bibliographies

Cook, Sybilla Avery. *Instructional Design for Libraries: An Annotated Bibliography*. New York: Garland, 1986.

Lockwood, Deborah L., comp. *Library Instruction: A Bibliography*. Westport, CT: Greenwood Press, 1980.

LOEX News, 1972-. See "To Read" section in each issue.

Rader, Hannelore B., comp. "Library Orientation and Instruction 1977-."
Annually in the April/May issue of *Reference Services Review*.

Handbooks and Training Textbooks

ACRL BIS Research Committee. *Evaluating Bibliographic Instruction*. Chicago: ACRL, 1983.

Adams, Mignon and Morris, Jacquelyn. *Teaching Library Skills for Academic Credit*. Phoenix, AZ: Oryx, 1985.

Beaubien, Anne, George, Mary, and Hogan, Sharon. *Learning the Library: Concepts and Methods for Effective Bibliographic Instruction*. NY: Bowker, 1982.

Breivik, Patricia Senn. *Planning the Library Instruction Program*. Chicago, IL: ALA, 1982.

Clark, Alice A. and Jones, Kay F. *Teaching Librarians to Teach*. Metuchen, NJ: Scarecrow Press, 1986.

Renford, Beverly and Hendrickson, Linnea. *Bibliographic Instruction: A Handbook*. NY: Neal-Schuman, 1981.

Rice, James G., Jr. *Teaching Library Use: A Guide for Library Instruction*. Westport, CT: Greenwood Press, 1981.

Roberts, Anne F. *Library Instruction for Librarians*. Littleton, CO: Libraries Unlimited, 1982.

Strauch, Katina and Oberman, Cerise. *Theories of Bibliographic Education: Designs for Teaching*. NY: Bowker, 1982.

Readings

Bibliographic Instruction in ARL Libraries. SPEC Kit #121. ARL Office of Management Studies, 1986.

Farber, Evan Ira. "The Importance of Teaching Use of the Library." *Library Issues: Briefings for Faculty and Administrators*. Vol. 2, no. 2, November 1981.

_____. "Teaching Use of the Library: Part II Implementation." *Library Issues*. Vol. 2, no. 3, January 1982.

Hardesty, Larry, Schmitt, John P., and Tucker, John Mark. *User Instruction in Academic Libraries: A Century of Selected Readings*. Metuchen, NJ: Scarecrow Press, 1986.

Katz, Bill and Fraley, Ruth A. *Library Instruction and Reference Services*. NY: Haworth Press, 1984.

Kirkendall, Carolyn, ed. "Library Instruction: A Column of Opinion." *Journal of Academic Librarianship*, 1976-1983; and "Dialogue and Debate a Column of Opinion." *Research Strategies*, 1983-1986.

LOEX Clearinghouse. Annual Library Instruction Conference/Workshop *Proceedings*, 1971-.

LOEX News. Vol. 1, no. 1, 1972-.

Lubans, John, Jr. *Educating the Library User*. NY: Bowker, 1974.

_____. *Educating the Public Library User*. Chicago: ALA, 1983.

_____. *Progress in Educating the Library User*. NY: Bowker, 1978.

_____. ed. "Library Literacy." *RQ*, 1980-1986.

Mellon, Constance, ed. *Bibliographic Instruction: The Second Generation*. Littleton, CO: Libraries Unlimited, 1987.

Mensching, Teresa Bungard, ed. "Dialogue and Debate A Column of Opinion." *Research Strategies*, 1986-.

COURSE-RELATED INSTRUCTION

Biggs, Mary Mancuso, and Weber, Mark. *Course-Related and Personalized Library Instruction.* Evansville, IN: University of Evansville, 1979. ED 172724.

Farber, Evan Ira. "Library Instruction Throughout the Curriculum: Earlham College Program." In *Educating the Library User*, edited by John Lubans, Jr., 145-162. NY: Bowker, 1974.

Kennedy, James R. "Integrated Library Instruction." *Library Journal* 95 (15 April 1970): 1450-1453.

Kennedy, James R., Jr., Kirk, Thomas G., and Weaver, G.A. "Course-related Library Instruction: A Case Study of the English and Biology Departments at Earlham College." *Drexel Library Quarterly* 7 (July-October 1971): 277-297.

Kirk, Thomas G. "Course-related Library Instruction in the 70's." In *Library Instruction in the Seventies: State of the Art*, edited by Hannelore B. Rader, 35-46. Ann Arbor, MI: Pierian Press, 1977.

Kirk, Thomas. *The Development of Course Related Library and Literature Use Instruction in Undergraduate Science Programs.* 1978. ED 152 230;-231; -232; -233.

Knapp, Patricia B. *An Experiment in Coordination Between Teaching and Library Staff for Changing Student Use of University Library Resources.* Detroit: Wayne State University, 1964.

————. "A Suggested Program of College Instruction in the Use of the Library." *Library Quarterly* 26 (1956): 224-231.

MacGregor, John, and McInnis, Raymond G. "Integrating Classroom Instruction and Library Research: The Cognitive Functions of Bibliographic Network Functions." *Journal of Higher Education* 48 (Jan-Feb 1977): 17-38.

McInnis, Raymond G. "Integrating Classroom Instruction and Library Research: An Essay Review." *Studies in History and Society* 4 (Winter 1974-75): 31-65.

Rodgers, Sharon. "Course-related Instruction for Sociology Students." In *Putting Library Instruction in its Place*, edited by Carolyn Kirkendall, 48-52. Ann Arbor, MI: Pierian Press, 1978.

Werking, Richard. "Course-related Instruction for History Majors." In *Putting Library Instruction in its Place: In the Library and in the Library School*, edited by Carolyn Kirkendall, 44-47. Ann Arbor, MI: Pierian Press, 1978.

CREDIT COURSES IN LIBRARY RESEARCH

Adams, Mignon S. and Morris, Jacquelyn M. *Teaching Library Skills for Academic Credit.* Phoenix, AZ: Oryz Press, 1985. 216p. $29.50. W/18 case studies.

Bales, Jack. "Library Instruction Course for Credit." *LIFline* News Sheet 26 (September 1984): 3-5.

Beaubien, Anne, Hogan, Sharon, and George, Mary. "Planning Courses." In *Learning the Library*, 199-216. New York: Bowker, 1982.

Clement, Russell T. and others. *Using the Joseph F. Smith Library.* 1981. ED 201 328. 2-hour course at Brigham Young University-Hawaii.

Doyen, Sally E. "A Study of Library Skills Instruction." *Top of the News* 38 (Fall 1981): 60-63.

Gavryck, Jacquelyn and others. *Library Research Curriculum Materials for a One-Credit Course.* 1981. ED 203 884. SUNY-Albany.

Englebrecht, Pamela. "Teaching the Credit Course: Pitfalls and Pleasures." *LIFline* News Sheet 19 (April 1982): 7-8.

Hales, Celia and Dianne Catlett. "Methololodogy: East Carolina University." *Research Strategies* 2 (Fall 1984): 156-165.

Hendrickson, Linnea and Renford, Beverly. "Credit Instruction." In *Bibliographic Instruction: A Handbook*, 121-134. New York: Neal-Schuman, 1980.

Kennedy, James. "Question: A Separate Course in Bibliography or Course-Related Library Instruction?" In *Library Orientation*, edited by Sul H. Lee, 18-28. Ann Arbor: Pierian Press, 1972.

Library Skills Course for EOP Students. ED 202 459. 1981. A 5-week course at SUNY-Plattsburgh.

McQuiston, Virginia Frank. "Measurement: Millikin University." *Research Strategies* 2 (Fall 1984): 166-171.

Morris, Jacquelyn M. "A Philosophical Defense of a Credit Course." In *Proceedings from the Second Southeastern Conference on Approaches to Bibliographic Instruction, ed. by Cerise Oberman-Soroka.* Charleston, SC: College of Charleston, 1980.

Reminick, Gerald. "Anatomy of a Library Course Proposal." *Community and Junior College Libraries* 1 (September 1983): 25-37.

Roberts, Anne. *A Study of Ten SUNY Campuses*

Offering an Undergraduate Credit Course in Library Instruction. ED 157 529. 1978.

Stewart, Frances. "Teaching Library Usage Through Programmed Instruction at Alabama A & M University." *The Alabama Librarian* 32 (November-December 1980): 8-11.

Sugranes, Mara R. and James A. Neal. "Evaluation of a Self-Paced Bibliographic Instruction Course." *College & Research Libraries* 44 (November 1983): 444-457.

Wood, Richard J. "The Impact of a Library Research Course on Students at Slippery Rock University." *Journal of Academic Librarianship* 10 (November 1984): 278-284.

MEDIATED LIBRARY INSTRUCTION: A LOEX BIBLIOGRAPHY

Adams, Mignon. "Bibliographic Instruction in Academic Libraries." *Catholic Library World* 52 (April 1981): 397-399.

Baldwin, Julia F. and Rudolph, R.S. "Improving Student Recall of Library Information from Slide/Tape Programs." *College & Research Libraries* 41 (January 1982): 78-80.

_____. "The Comparative Effectiveness of a Slide/Tape Show and a Library Tour." *College & Research Libraries* 38 (January 1979): 31-35.

Ferralli, Anthony and Kathryn. "Interactive Video: A Tool for Changing Times." *Media and Methods* 22 (1986): 10-13.

Freedman, Janet and Bently, Harold. "Slide Tape Programs." In *Information Seeking.* Metuchen, NJ: Scarecrow Press, 1982.

Hall, John B. and Leeper, D.P. "Mediated Approaches to Bibliographic Instruction." *Drexel Library Quarterly* 16 (January 1980): Issue.

Hardesty, Larry. *The Use of Slide/Tape Presentations in Academic Libraries.* NY: Jeffrey Norton, 1978.

Jacobson, Gertrude N. and Albright, M.J. "Motivation Via Videotape: Keys to Undergraduate Library Instruction in the Research Library." *Journal of Academic Librarianship* 9 (November 1983): 270-274.

Lamkin, Bernice. "Media Center for the 21st Century." *School Library Journal* 33 (November 1986): 25-29.

Lolley, John L. "Videotape Programs." *Drexel Library Quarterly* 16 (January 1980): 83-102.

Lolley, John L. and Watkins, Ruth. "The Use of Audio-Visuals in Developing Favorable Attitudes Toward Library Instruction." *Educational Technology* (January 1979): 56-58.

McNeil, Don W. *Academic Library Instruction: The Use of Films,....Educational Television,....Audio Learning,....Programmed Learning,....Visual Learning Material.* 1980. ED 190 135.

Orgren, Carl F. *Production of Slide/Tape Programs.* Iowa City: University of Iowa, 1972.

Palmer, Millicent C. "Creating Slide/Tape Library Instruction: The Librarian's Role." *Drexel Library Quarterly* 8 (July 1972): 251-267.

Payne, John H. "The Plan is the Design-Preparation for an Audiovisual Script." *Colorado Libraries* 9 (June 1983): 37-38.

Renford, Beverly and Henrickson, Linnea. "Audiovisual Materials and Equipment." In *Bibliographic Instruction: A Handbook.* NY: Neal-Schuman, 1980.

Rosenblum, Joseph. "Toward an Alternative to the In-house Tour." *Southeastern Librarian* 28 (Winter 1978): 235-238.

Utz, Peter. "Producing AV for Library Instruction and Living to Tell About It." *New Jersey Libraries* 17 (Fall 1984): 28-31.

Violette, Judith L. "Library Instruction With Slides and Slide/Tapes." In *Improving Library Instruction:*

How to Teach and How to Evaluate, edited by Carolyn Kirkendall. Ann Arbor: Pierian Press, 1979.

Wells, J., Sanders, A., and Trinklein, D. *Creating a Videotape for Instruction*. Columbia, MO: University of Missouri, 1985.

EVALUATION OF BIBLIOGRAPHIC INSTRUCTION: A LOEX BIBLIOGRAPHY

Adams, Mignon. "Effects of Evaluation of Teaching Methods." In *Improving Library Instruction: How to Teach and How to Evaluate*, edited by Carolyn Kirkendall, 97-100. Ann Arbor, MI: Pierian Press, 1979.

American Library Association. Association of College and Research Libraries Bibliographic Instruction Section. Research Committee. *Bibliographic Instruction Evaluation Handbook*. Chicago: ACRL, 1984.

Beeler, Richard J., ed. *Evaluating Library Instruction*. Ann Arbor, MI: Pierian Press, 1975.

Bloomfield, Masse. "Testing for Library-use Competence." In *Educating the Library User*, edited by John Lubans, Jr., 221-231. New York: Bowker, 1974.

Breivik, Patricia. "Evaluation." In *Planning the Library Program*, 94-108. Chicago: ALA, 1982.

Burton, Susan. "Objective Tests as an Evaluation Tool: Problems in Construction and Use." In *Library Instruction in the Seventies: State of the Art*, edited by Hannelore B. Rader, 99-103. Ann Arbor, MI: Pierian Press, 1977.

Freedman, Janet L. and Bantley, Harold A. "Does It Work? Program Evaluation," in *Information Searching: A Handbook for Designing and Creating Instructional Programs*, 178-184. Rev ed. Metuchen, NJ: Scarecrow Press, 1982.

Frick, Elizabeth. "Evaluating Student Knowledge of Facilities." In *Improving Library Instruction: How to Teach and How to Evaluate*, edited by Carolyn A. Kirkendall, 101-106. Ann Arbor, MI: Pierian Press, 1979.

Glogoff, Stuart. "Using Statistical Tests to Evaluate Library Instruction Sessions." *Journal of Academic Librarianship* 4 (January 1979): 438-442.

Hardesty, Larry, et al. "Evaluating Library-use Instruction." *College & Research Libraries* 40 (July

1979): 309-317.

Kaplowitz, Joan. "Pre- and Post-test Evaluation of the English 3 Library Instruction Program at UCLA." *Research Strategies* 4 (Winter 1986): 11-17.

King, David N. and Ory, John C. "Effects of Library Instruction on Student Research: A Case Study." *College & Research Libraries* 42 (January 1981): 31-41.

Kirk, Thomas G. "Evaluation of Library Orientation and Instruction Programs: A Taxonomy." In *Planning and Developing a Library Orientation Program*, edited by Mary Bolner, 41-51. Ann Arbor, MI: Pierian Press: 1975.

Lubans, John. "Evaluating Library-user Education Programs." In *Educating the Library User*, edited by John Lubans, 232-253. New York: Bowker, 1974.

Nagy, Lasio A. and Thomas, Martha Lou. "An Evaluation of the Teaching Effectiveness of Two Library Instructional Videotapes." *College and Research Libraries* 42 (January 1981): 26-30.

Olevnik, Peter P. "Evaluation as a tool for Program Development." In *Improving Library Instruction: How to Teach and How to Evaluate*, edited by Carolyn Kirkendall, 107-111. Ann Arbor, MI: Pierian Press, 1979.

Paterson, Ellen R. "An Assessment of College Student Library Skills." *RQ* 17 (Spring 1978): 226-229.

Person, Roland. "Long Term Evaluation of Bibliographic of Instruction: Lasting Encouragement." *College & Research Libraries* 42 (January 1981): 19-25.

Rice, James, Jr. "Testing and Evaluation." In *Teaching Library Use: A Guide for Library Instruction*, 97-129. Westport, CT: Greenwood Press, 1981.

Roberts, Anne F. "Measuring the Results." In L

Library Instruction for Librarians, by A. Roberts, 84-89. Littleton, CO: Libraries Unlimited, 1982.

Robinson, Tracey D. and Drott, M. Carl. "Student Book Reports: Some Objective Measurements." *Catholic Library World* 52 (September 1980): 57-59.

Talar, Anita. "User Needs as Viewed by the User: Asking Students What They Need from the Library." *New Jersey Libraries* 17 (Fall 1984): 14-21.

Werking, Richard. "Evaluating Bibliographic Education: A Review and Critique." *Library Trends* 29 (Summer 1980): 153-172.

_____. "The Place of Evaluation in Bibliographic Education." In *Proceedings from the Southeastern Conference on Approaches to Bibliographic Instruction*, edited by Cerise Oberman-Soroka, 100-118. Charleston, SC: College of Charleston, 1978.

COMPUTER-ASSISTED LIBRARY INSTRUCTION: A LOEX BIBLIOGRAPHY

Aken, Rob and Olson, Laura. "Computer-Assisted Instruction in Academic Libraries." *Journal of Computer-Based Instruction* 13 (Summer 1986): 94-97.

Arnott, Pat. "Computer-Assisted Bibliographic Instruction: The University of Delaware Experience." *Crossroads: Proceedings of the First National ITA Conference*, October 1984.

Arnott, Patricia and Richards, Deborah E. "Using the IBM Personal Computer for Library Instruction." *Reference Services Review* 13 (Spring 1985): 69-72.

Clark, Alice S. "Computer-Assisted Library Instruction." In *Educating the Library User*, edited by John Lubans, Jr, 336-349. New York: Bowker, 1974.

Culkin, Patricia B. "CAI Experiment." *American Libraries* 23 (June 1972): 643-645.

_____. "Computer-Assisted Instruction in Library Use." *Drexel Library Quarterly* 8 (July 1972): 301-311.

_____. "Computer-Based Public Access Systems: A Forum for Library Instruction." *Drexel Library Quarterly* 16 (January 1980): 69-82.

Eastmond, J. Nicholls, Jr. *An Evaluation of Computer Assisted Instruction in the Merrill Library at Utah*. 1975. ED 112 880.

Fitzgerald, Patricia A., Arnott, Patricia, and Richards, Deborah. "Computer-Assisted Instruction in Libraries: Guidelines for Effective Lesson Design." *Library Hi Tech* 14 (Summer 1986): 29-37.

Gratch, Bonnie. "Computer-Assisted Instruction: An Unfulfilled Promise." *Wilson Library Bulletin* 61 (December 1986): 20-22.

Hansen, Lois N. "Computer-Assisted Instruction in Library Use: An Evaluation." *Drexel Library Quarterly* 8 (July 1972): 345-355.

Hendley, Gaby G. *Using the Microcomputer to Generate Materials for Bibliographic Instruction*. 1984. ED 252 190.

Huston-Miyamoto, Mary. "Computer-Assisted Instruction in Libraries: Past, Present, and Future." In *Directions for the Decade: Library Instruction in the 1980's*, edited by Carolyn Kirkendall, 99-118. Ann Arbor, MI: Pierian Press, 1980.

Johnson, Kathleen A. and Plake, Barbara S. "Evaluation of PLATO Library Instruction Lessons: Another View." *Journal of Academic Librarianship* 6 (July 1980): 154-158.

Lawrence, Gail Herndon. "The Computer as an Instructional Device: New Directions for Library User Education." *Library Trends* 29 (Summer 1980): 139-152.

Lubans, John. "Computers and User Education: A Misalliance." *RQ* 24 (Winter 1984): 135-137.

Machalow, Robert. *Computer Based Library Orientation*. ED 252 239.

Mosely, Patricia and Jackson R. "A Console That Loves to Teach Library Basics." *American Libraries* 15 (September 1984): 593.

Nelson, Ilene. "The Computer: Cure-all or Snake Oil?" *RQ* 23 (Fall 1983): 7-8.

Ross, J.E. "Microsoftware for Library Skills Instruction." *School Library Journal* 31 (November 1984): 68-73.

Smith, Lotsee and Swisser, K. "Microcomputers in School Library Media Centers." *Drexel Library Quarterly* 20 (Winter 1984): 7-15.

Starks, David D., Horn, Barbara J., and Slavens, Thomas P. "Two Modes of Computer-Assisted Instruction in a Library Reference Course." *Journal of the American Society for Information Science* 23 (July-August 1972): 271-277.

Sugranes, Maria R., and Benson-Talley, Lois. "Computer-Assisted Instruction Remediation Program for Credit Course in Bibliographic Instruction." *Research Strategies* 4 (Winter 1986): 18-26.

Thompson, Glenn J. "Computer Use in LMED 100, How to Use the Library." *C&RL News* 45 (February 1984): 83.

Tobin, Carol, et al. "The Computer and Library Instruction." *Reference Services Review* 12 (Winter 1984): 71-78.

Walker, Elizabeth and Culkin, Patricia. "Computer-Assisted Instruction in Academic Libraries." In *Proceedings: Third International Conference on Library User Education*, edited by Peter Fox and Ian Malley, 126-135. Loughborough: INFUSE, 1983.

Williams, Mitsuko and Davis, Elizabeth B. "Computer-Assisted Instruction: An Overview." In *Theories of Bibliographic Education: Designs for Teaching*, by Cerise Oberman and Katina Strauch, 171-191. New York: Bowker, 1982.

Wilson, Wayne. "Computer-Assisted Instruction in an Academic Library." *Information Technology and Libraries* 2 (December 1983): 389-393.

Wood, Richard J. *A Computer-Assisted Instruction Program on How to Use a Library Card Catalog: Description, Program, and Evaluation.* 1975. ED 167 156.

USING WORKBOOKS IN BIBLIOGRAPHIC INSTRUCTION: A LOEX BIBLIOGRAPHY

Dudley, Miriam. "Of Workbooks and Whirlwinds." In *Library Use Education: Are New Approaches Needed?*, edited by Peter K. Fox. BLRD Report no. 5503. London: British Library, 1980.

_____. "The State of Library Instruction Credit Courses and the State of the Use of Library Skills Workbooks." In *Library Instruction in the Seventies: State of the Art*, edited by Hannelore B. Rader, 79-84. Ann Arbor, MI: Pierian Press, 1977.

Jewell, Timothy D. "Student Reactions to a Self-Paced Library Skills Workbook Program: Survey Evidence." *College & Research Libraries* 43 (September 1983): 371-378.

Kenney, Patricia Ann and McArthur, Judith N. "Designing and Evaluating a Programmed Library Instruction Text." *College & Research Libraries* 45 (January 1984): 35-42.

Mertin, Barbara. "The Self-paced Workbook in Teaching Basic Library Skills." In Bibliographic Instruction, 1977 Conference, West Virginia Library Association. Bethany, WV: WVLA, 1977. ED 144 582.

Mitchel, Marguerite. "The Library Skills Workbook at Stephens College." *Show-Me Libraries* 32 (January 1981): 32-33.

Nash, Vivien. "Workbooks in Library Skills - Palliative, Panacea of Placebo?: In *Proceedings: Third International Conference on Library User Education*, edited by Peter Fox and Ian Malley, 126-135. (Loughborough: INFUSE, 1983).

Phipps, Shelley, and Dickstein, Ruth. "The Library Skills Program at the University of Arizona." *Journal of Academic Librarianship* 5 (September 1979): 205-214.

Phipps, Shelley. "Why Use Workbooks? or Why Do the Chickens Cross the Road? An Other Metaphor, Mixed." *Drexel Library Quarterly* 16 (January 1980): 39-51.

Pryor, Judith M. "The Case for Workbook Instruction." In *Proceedings from the Second Southeastern Conference on Approaches to Bibliographic Instruction*, edited by Cerise Oberman-Soroka. Charleston, SC: College of Charleston, 1980.

Renford, Beverly. "Self-paced Program for Beginning College Students." *Journal of Academic Librarianship* 4 (September 1978): 200-203.

Renford, Beverly and Hendrickson, Linnea. "Library Skills Workbooks." In *Bibliographic Instruction: A Handbook*, 97-120. New York: Neal-Schuman, 1980.

Stoffle, Carla J. "The Subject-Workbook Approach to Teaching Discipline-related Library Research

Skills." In *Library User Education: Are New Approaches Needed?*, edited by Peter K. Fox. BLRD Report no. 5503. London: British Library, 1980.

Suprenant, Thomas T. "Learning Theory, Lecturer and Programmed Instruction Text: An Experiment in Bibliographic Instruction." *College & Research Libraries* 43 (January 1982): 31-37.

Villar, Susanne and Emmons, Paul. "Using the Computer to Randomize Questions for Library Instruction Worksheets." *Research Strategies* 1 (Spring 1983): 52-57.

Voit, Beth and Tribble, Joan. "The Workbook Approach to Teaching Basic Library Skills in the Community College: Two Points of View." *Kentucky Library Association Bulletin* 44 (Winter 1980): 4-8.

Ware, Susan A. and Morganti, Deena J. "A Competency Based Approach to Assessing Workbook Effectiveness." *Research Strategies* 4 (Winter 1986): 4-10.

White, Donald J. "Workbooks for Basic Library Instruction." *Canadian Library Journal* 38 (August 1981): 213-219.

LIBRARY SKILLS WORKBOOKS IN ERIC

Adams, Barbara and Graves, Gail. *The Library Workbook. A Research Guide.* Rev. 1985. ED 264 876.

Baum, Nathan, et al. *Introduction to the Stony Brook Library: A Self-Paced Workbook for INT 150.* 1984. ED 269 038.

Bhullar, Pushpajit and Hosel, Harold. *Library Skills.* 1979. ED 190 083.

Biglin, Karen, et. al. *Your NAU Library Workbook.* 1981. ED 194 117.

Bousfield, Wendy, et al. *An Introduction to SULIRS and the Card Catalog. Workbook and Instruction Manual.* 1984. ED 264 875.

Bryan, Barton B. and Rizzo, Joseph. *Finding Biomedical Information. A Learning Module for Medical Technology Students on the Basis of the Use of Medical Literature in the Shiffman Medical Library, Wayne State University, Detroit, Michigan.* 1982. ED 229 046.

Bryson, Emily Montez and Dale, Roland. *Library Research Manual: The Health Sciences.* 1981. ED 216 853.

Bryson, Emily M. and Kelly, Alter. *Library Research Manual: History.* 1982. ED 229 011.

Dew, Stephen H. *Technical Writing: Library Resources for Engineers. A Self-Paced Workbook for the University of Arkansas Libraries.* Rev. 1985. ED 265 882.

Ellsbury, Susan. *Library Instruction Workbook for the Sciences.* 1980. ED 210 028.

Flower, Clara. *Finding a Book: The Card Catalog. Library Instruction Series. Unit II.* 1979. ED 162 666.

Flower, Clara K. *Finding an Article: Indexes and Abstracts. Library Instruction Series. Unit III.* 1979. ED 162 666.

_____. *Finding Your Way: Orientation to the Library. Library Instruction Series. Unit I.* 1979. ED 162 664.

Gebhard, Patricia and Silver, Barbara. *Library Skills: A Self-Paced Workbook.* 1979. ED 167 133.

Gibson, Mary J. and Kaczmarke, Mildred. *Student Activity Workbook for Use with Finding Information in the Library.* 1979. ED 161 461.

Hallman, Clark N. *A Library Instruction Program for Beginning Undergraduates.* 1980. ED 188 633.

Hodina, Alfred, et al. *Information Resources in the Sciences and Engineering. A Laboratory Workbook.* 1981. ED 205 178.

Hostettler, John D., et al. *Chemical Literature Exercises and Resources (CLEAR).* 1982. ED 219 266.

Jenkins, Kathleen H. *The Library Skills Learning Package: An Evaluation.* 1981. ED 195 277.

Lyle, Stanley P. and Ashbough, Donald. *Library Skills and Resources for Business Research.* 1982. ED 216 696.

Morrison, Ray and Nolen, Terrence. *Library Skills*

Workbook. 1982. ED 233 726.

Pikoff, Howard. *Workbook for Library Research in Psychology.* 1978. ED 151 025.

Pritchard, Eileen. *Library and Classroom Exercises in Science.* 1980. ED 188 910.

Renford, Beverly. *Library Resources: A Self-Paced Workbook.* Rev. 1985. ED 269 025.

Rice, Shiela. *Workbook for the Introduction to the Library.* 1979. ED 163 953.

Smalley, Topsy. *Basic Reference Tools for Nursing Research. A Workbook with Explanations and Examples.* 1981. ED 197 071.

Trithart, David. *Library Resources in Education: An Introductory Module for Students and Teachers.* 1976. ED 124 129.

Using the Madonna College Library: A Self-Instructional Library Orientation. 1980. ED 233 719.

Wright, Nancy. *Workbook in Library Skills.* 1981. ED 208 915-918.

TEACHING THE TEACHER - LIBRARIAN: A BIBLIOGRAPHY JOAN ORMONDROYD 1986

Adams, Mignon S. and Jacquelyn M. Morris. *Teaching Library Skills for Academic Credit.* Phoenix: Oryx, 1985.

Annual Conference of the American Library Association ACRL Bibliographic Instruction Section. *Back to the Books: Bibliographic Instruction and the Theory of Information Source.* Chicago, ALA, 1983.

Baldwin, Julia F. and Robert S. Rudolph. "Comparative Effectiveness of a Slide/Tape Show and a Library Tour." *College and Research Libraries* 40 (January 1979): 31-35.

Breivik, Patricia S. "The Neglected Horizon: An Expanded Education Role for Academic Libraries," 220-232. *New Horizons for Academic Libraries.* New York: K.G. Saur, 1979.

Budd, John. "Librarians are Teachers." *Library Journal* 107 (15 October 1982): 1944-1946.

Clark, Alice S. and Kay F. Jones. *Teaching Librarians to Teach: On-the-Job Training for Bibliographic Instruction Librarians.* Metuchen: Scarecrow, 1986.

Conference on Library Orientation for Academic Libraries, Eastern Michigan University, May 8-9, 1980. *Directions for the Decade; Library Instructions in the 1980s.* Ann Arbor: Pierian, 1981.

Conference on Library Orientation for Academic Libraries, Eastern Michigan University, May 6-7 1982. *Bibliographic Instruction and the Learning Process; Theory, Style, and Motivation.* Ann Arbor: Pierian, 1984.

Culkin, Patricia B. "Computer-Based Public Access Systems: A Forum for Library Instruction." *Drexel*

Library Quarterly 16 (January 1980): 69-82.

Ford, James E. "The Natural Alliance Between Librarians and English Teachers in Course-Related Library Use Instruction." *College and Research Libraries* (September 1982): 379-384.

Frey, A.L. and S. Spigel. "Educating Adult Users in the Public Library." *Library Journal* (15 April 1979): 894-896.

Graef, Jean I. and Larry Greenwood. "Marketing Library Services: A Case Study in Providing Bibliographic Instruction in an Academic Library." *New Horizons for Academic Libraries,* 212-228. New York: K.G. Saur, 1979.

Guskin, Alan E., Carla Stoffle, and Joe Boisse. "The Academic Library as a Teaching Library: A Role for the 1980's." *Library Trends* 28 (Fall 1979): 281-296.

Hogan, Sharon A. "Training and Education of Library Instruction Librarians." *Library Trends* 29 (Summer 1980): 105-126.

Kirk, Thomas G. "Course-Related Library and Literature Use Instruction: An Attempt to Develop Model Programs." *New Horizons for Academic Libraries,* 268-276. New York: K.G. Saur, 1979.

Kobelski, Pamela and Mary Reichel. "Conceptual Frameworks for Bibliographic Instruction." *Journal of Academic Librarianship* 7 (May 1981): 73-77.

Kuhlthau, Carol Collier. *Teaching the Library Research Process: A Step-By-Step Program for Secondary School Students.* West Nyack: Center for Applied Research in Education, 1985.

Leerburger, Benedict A. *Marketing the Library.*

White Plains: Knowledge Industry, 1982.

Lubans, John Jr. *Educating the Library User.* New York: Bowker, 1974.

MacGregory, John and Raymond G. McInnis. "Integrating Classroom Instruction and Library Research: The Cognitive Functions of Bibliographic Network Structures." *Journal of Higher Education*, XLVIII, 1 (January/February 1977): 17-38.

Oberman, Cerise and Katina Struach, eds. *Theories of Bibliographic Instruction: Designs for Teaching.* New York: Bowker, 1982.

Palmer, Millicent. "Creating Slide-tape Library Instruction: The Librarian's Role." *Drexel Library Quarterly* 8 (July 1972): 251-266.

Ramey, M. and A. Spanjer. "Videotaping Bibliographic Instruction: A Confrontation with Self." *Research Strategies* 2 (Spring 1984): 71-75.

Renford, Beverly L. "A Self-Paced Workbook Program for Beginning College Students." *Journal of Academic Librarianship* 4 (September 1978): 200-203.

Roberts, Anne. *Library Instruction for Librarians.* Littleton, CO: Libraries Unlimited, Inc., 1982.

Rogers, Sharon. "Research Strategies: Bibliographic Instruction for Undergraduates." *Library Trends* 29 (Summer 1980): 69-81.

Smalley, T.N. "Bibliographic Instruction in Academic Libraries: Questioning Some Assumptions." *Journal of Academic Librarianship* 3 (November 1977): 280-283.

Smith, Terry C. *Making Successful Presentations: A Self-Teaching Guide.* New York: Wiley Press, 1984.

Surprenant, Thomas T. "Learning Theory, Lecture, and Programmed Instruction Text: An Experiment in Bibliographic Instruction." *College and Research Libraries* 43 (January 1982): 31-37.

Tucker, J.M. "User Education in American Libraries: A Century in Retrospect." *Library Trends* 29 (Summer 1980): 9-27.

Vincent, C. Paul. "Bibliographic Instruction and the Reference Desk: A Symbiotic Relationship." In Katz, Bill and Fraley, Ruth A. eds. *Library Instruction and Reference Services*, 39-47. NY: Hawthorne Press, 1984.

Werking, Richard H. "Evaluating Bibliographic Education: A Review and Critique." *Library Trends* 29 (Summer 1980): 105-126.

White, Herbert S., ed. *Education for Professional Librarians.* White Plains: Knowledge Industry, 1986.

Young, Arthur P. "And Gladly Teach: Bibliographic Instruction and the Library." *Advances in Librarianship* 10 Academic Press 1980: 63-88.

Participants

Sponsored by the LOEX Clearinghouse and Ohio State University--7-8 May 1987

Steve Aby
Northeastern University
201 Dodge Library
Boston, MA 02115

Barbara Kay Adams
University of Mississippi
J.D. Williams Library
University, MS 38677

Mignon Adams
Philadelphia College of Pharmacy and Science
42nd & Woodland
Philadelphia, PA 19104

Diane L. Allen
Fort Lewis College Library
Durango, CO 81301

Bruce Andrew
Buffalo State College
1300 Elmwood Ave.
Buffalo, NY 14305

Vickie Anway
Roanoke College Library
212 High St.
Salem, VA 24153

Mary Ellen Armentrout
Adrian College
Shipman Library
Adrian, MI 49221

Mary Jo Arnold
The Ohio State University
112 Caldwell
2024 Neil Ave.
Columbus, OH 43210

Helen M. Barber
PO Box 3475
Las Cruces, NM 88003

Richard Bell
McIntyre Library
University of Wisconsin-Eau Claire
Eau Claire, WI 54702-4004

James A. Belz
University of Wisconsin
Stevens Point
University Library
Stevens Point, WI 54481

Donna G. Bentley
W.C. Jackson Library
UNC-Greensboro
Greensboro, NC 27412

Ann Bevilacqua
New York University
Bobst Library
70 Washington Sq. South
New York, NY 10012

Eleanor S. Block
The Ohio State University
100 Journalism Bldg.
242 W. 18th
Columbus, OH 43210

Julie Bobay
Indiana University
Library E172
Bloomington, IN 47405

Dana W. Boden
Helm Library 104B
Western Kentucky University
Bowling Green, KY 42101

Dorita F. Bolger
Westminister College
Market St.
New Wilmington, PA 16172

Karen Bordonaro
Canisius College Library
Reference Library
2001 Main St.
Buffalo, NY 14208

Patrick C. Boyden
Kent State University
Library Building
Kent, OH 44242

Pamela Bradigan
OSU Health Sciences Library
376 W. 10th Ave.
Columbus, OH 43210

Teresa Bungard
Eastern Michigan University
Library
Ypsilanti, MI 48197

Mary-Beth Bunge
The Ohio State University
326 Main Library
1858 Neil Ave. Mall
Columbus, OH 43210

Jane Caldwell
Emory & Henry College
Kelly Library
Emory, VA 24327

Jody L. Caldwell
SUNY Brockport
Drake Library
Brockport, NY 14420

Lynn Cameron
James Madison University
Library
Harrisonburg, VA 22807

Douglas G. Campbell
Northwestern Michigan College
Mark Osterlin Library
Traverse City, MI 49684

Gabrielle Carr
Indiana University Southeast
4201 Grant Line Rd.
New Albany, IN 47150

Michele Cash
Indiana University
Library
PO Box 7111
1700 Mishawaka Ave.
South Bend, IN 46634

Thomas J. Cashore
University of Nebraska
Love Library
Lincoln, NE 68588

Tommy A. Clark
Valdosta State College Library
Valdosta, GA 31698

Margit Codispoti
Indiana University
2101 Coliseum Blvd. East
Fort Wayne, IN 46805

Helen Coffey
Queen's University
Douglas Library
Kingston, Ontario

Laurie Cohen
207 Hillman Library
University of Pittsburgh
Pittsburgh, PA 15260

Keith M. Cottam
The University of Wyoming
PO Box 3334 University Station
Laramie, WY 82070

Nancy Courtney
University of Dayton Research Library
300 College Park
Dayton, OH 45469

William J. Crowe
The Ohio State University
1858 Neil Ave. Mall
Columbus, OH 43210

Jean M. Crowley
Marymount University
Ireton Library
2807 North Glebe Rd.
Arlington, VA 22207

Kay Cutler
Virginia Commonwealth University
Cabell Library
901 Park Ave.
Richmond, VA 23284

Scott Davis
Indiana State University
Cunningham Library
Terre Haute, IN 47809

Trisha L. Davis
Ohio Wesleyan University
Audio-visual Services
Beeghly Library
Delaware, OH 43015

Susan H. DeGregory
University of North Alabama
PO Box 5230
Florence, AL 35632-0001

Mary Karen Delmont
State University College, Buffalo
1300 Elmwood Ave.
Buffalo, NY 14222

Amy L. DiBartolo
State University College, Buffalo
E.H. Butler Library
1300 Elmwood Ave.
Buffalo, NY 14222

Maria Dittman
Marquette University Library
1415 W. Wisconsin Ave.
Milwaukee, WI 53233

Linda J. Durfee
Wessell Library
Tufts University
Medford, MA 02155

Paula Elliot
Holland Library
Washington State University
Pullman, WA 99164-5610

Eugene A. Engeldinger
McIntyre Library
University of Wisconsin-Eau Claire
Eau Claire, WI 54702-4004

Susan M. Falgner
4701 Delhi Rd.
Mount St. Joseph, OH 45051

Jill B. Fatzer
Ohio State Libraries
1858 Neil Ave.
Columbus, OH 43210

Faye A. Flesia
UWC-Waukesha
1500 University Dr.
Waukesha, WI 53188

Marietta Frank
Xavier College
3800 Victory Parkway
Cincinnati, OH 45207

Paul Frantz
University of Oregon
284B, Main Library
Eugene, OR 97403

Elaine Franz
St. Andrews Presbyterian
De Tamble Library
Laurinburg, NC 28352

William J. Frost
Bloomsburg University
Bloomsburg, PA 17815

Tara Lynn Fulton
E.M. Cudahy Library
Loyola University of Chicago
6525 N. Sheridan Rd.
Chicago, IL 60626

Kathy M. Gaynor
Friends University
Edmund Stanley Library
2100 University Ave.
Wichita, KS 67213

Eva Godwin
Ohio State University
Main Library
1858 Neil Ave. Mall
Columbus, OH 43210

Denise Green
University of Toledo
Carlson Library
2801 West Bancroft
Toledo, OH 43606

Marcia Grimes
Wheaton College
Norton, MA 02766

Margaret Groesbeck
Amherst College Library
Amherst, MA 01002

Christine Hannon
Bracken Library
Ball State University
Muncie, IN 47306

Dorothy Herbert
MPLS Community College
1501 Hennepin Ave.
Minneapolis, MN 55403

Randall Hoelzen
Adams State College Library
Alamosa, CO 81102

Barbara Howes
Butler University
Irwin Library
4600 Sunset Ave.
Indianapolis, IN 46208

Stephen L. Hupp
University of Detroit
4001 West McNichols Rd.
Detroit, MI 48221

Irene W. Hurlbert
University of California
Central University Library
La Jolla, CA 92093

Janet Hurlbert
Lycoming College Library
Williamsport, PA 17001

Carol A. Hustuft
Concordia College
Moorhead, MN 56560

Dave Johnson
The Ohio State University Libraries
Columbus, OH 43210

Judy Ann Johnson
Cedarville College
PO Box 601
Cedarville, OH 45314

Lisa Johnson
Hiram College
Reference Library/BI Coord.
Hiram, OH 44234

Liz Benson Johnson
University of Minnesota
10 University Dr.
Duluth, MN 55812

Deborah Jones
Butler University
Irwin Library
4600 Sunset Ave.
Indianapolis, IN 46208

Michael Kasper
Amherst College Library
Amherst, MA 01002

Becky Kelien
Indiana University Southeast
4201 Grant Line Rd.
Box 679
New Albany, IN 47150

Barbara E. Kemp
Washington State University Library
Pullman, WA 99164-5610

Harris W. Kennedy
University of Southern Maine Library
96 Falmouth St.
Portland, ME 04103

Mary P. Key
The Ohio State University
2120 Fyffe Rd.
Columbus, OH 43210

Carolyn Kirkendall
Eastern Michigan University
Room 217C-Library
Ypsilanti, MI 48197

Becky Kornegay
Hunter Library
Western Carolina University
Cullowhee, NC 28723

Kathleen Krause
Roesch Library
University of Dayton
300 College Park
Dayton, OH 45469

Jay Ladd
The Ohio State University
1858 Neil Ave. Mall
Columbus, OH 43210

Linda Lawrence
University of Delaware Library
Newark, DE 19717

Julie Long
St. Mary's College
Cushwa-Leighton Library
Notre Dame, IN 46556

Patricia Lynn
Wayne State University
Perdy-Kresge Library
Detroit, MI 48202

Janice Marie
Regis College
2330 Robinson St.
Colorado Springs, CO 80904

Rosetta P. Martin
Trident Technical College
PO Box 10367
Charleston, SC 29411

Linda Masselink
Davenport College
435 East Fulton
Grand Rapids, MI 49503

Diane Matyjasik
West Virginia University
Evansdale Library
Morgantown, WV 26506-6105

Nancy McClements
University of Wisconsin
Instructional Materials Ctr.
225 North Mills St. Room 368
Madison, WI 53706

Tom McNally
The Ohio State University Libraries
Columbus, OH 43210

James S. McPhee
University of Nevada
4505 Maryland Parkway
Las Vegas, NV 89154

Patricia Mehok
Montgomery College
51 Mannakee St.
Rockville, MD 20850

Gloria B. Meisel
Westchester Community
75 Grasslands Rd.
Valhalla, NY 10595

Marsha A. Miller
Indiana State University
Cunningham Library
Terre Haute, IN 47809

Sally Jo Milne
Goshen College
Good Library
Goshen, IN 46526

Annette M. Monaco
Le Moyne College Library
Le Moyne Hts.
Syracuse, NY 14314

Janet Mongan
Cleveland State University Library
1860 East 22nd St.
Cleveland, OH 44115

Kathryn Moore
University of NC at Greensboro
Jackson Library
Greensboro, NC 27412

Linda Moore
Hillsdale College
Hillsdale, MI 49242

Carol Mularski
The Ohio State University
Health Sciences Library
376 West 10th Ave.
Columbus, OH 43210

Fred Musto
Indiana University
Main Library
Bloomington, IN 47405

Gwenn Neville
Millikin University
1184 W. Main St.
Library
Decatur, IL 62522

Marianne Nolan
Cleveland State University
1983 East 24th St.
Cleveland, OH 44115

Marsha L. Nolf
Louis L. Manderino Library
California, PA 15419

Emily M. Okada
Indiana University-Undergraduate Library
Main Library, W121
Bloomington, IN 47405

Joan Ormondroyd
Cornell University
Uris Undergraduate Library
Reference Department
Ithaca, NY 14853

Richard Page
University of New Mexico
Reference Department
Zimmerman Library
Albuquerque, NM 87131

Mary Pagliero Popp
Undergraduate Library
Library W121
Indiana University
Bloomington, IN 47405

Carol A. Patrick
Cleveland State University
1860 East 22nd St.
Cleveland, OH 44115

Susan Phillips
Ohio University
Chillicothe Library
Box 629
Chillicothe, OH 45601

Mary I. Piette
Utah State University
Merrill Library, Reference
Logan, UT 84322

Molly Pitts
Berea College
Hutchins Library
Berea, KY 40404

Rosario Poli
Case Western Reserve University
11161 East Blvd.
Cleveland, OH 44106

Audrey Potter
Wheelock College Library
132 The Riverway
Boston, MA 02215

Jill H. Powell
Cornell University
Engineering Library
Carpenter Hall
Ithaca, NY 14853

Ann Power
The University of Alabama
PO Box S
Tuscaloosa, AL 35487

Cheryl A. Price
Galvin Library
Illinois Institute of Technology
Chicago, IL 60616

Janet E. Pursel
Bowling Green State University
Jerome Library-Information Service
Bowling Green, OH 43403

Marty Reimers
Butler Community College
Reference & Media Service Library
Oak Hills
Butler, PA 16001

Teresa Reynolds
Indiana University Southeast
4201 Grant Line Rd.
New Albany, IN 47150

Trish Ridgeway
University of Pennsylvania
Van Pelt Library
Philadelphia, PA 19104

Albert F. Riess
SUNY at Buffalo State College
Butler Library
1300 Elmwood Ave.
Buffalo, NY 14222

Betty Lee Ronayne
Milton S. Eisenhower Library
Johns Hopkins University
3400 North Charles St.
Baltimore, MD 21218

Roberta L. Ruben
Western Illinois University
Horrabin Hall 39
Macomb, IL 61455

Margaret Ruddy
Cardinal Stritch College Library
6801 North Yates Rd.
Milwaukee, WI 53217

Christina Russell
Community College of Allegheny County
808 Ridge Ave.
Pittsburgh, PA 15212

Natalie B. Rutledge
West Virginia University
Evansdale Library
Morgantown, WV 26506-6105

Edmund F. SantaVicca
Cleveland State University
1860 East 22nd St.
Cleveland, OH 44115

Mara Saule
University of Vermont
Bailey/Howe Library
Burlington, VT 05405

Nan Schichtel
Aquinas College
Woodhouse LRC-1607
Robinson Road SE
Grand Rapids, MI 49506

Roger Sell
The Ohio State University
Inst. Development & Evaluation
Columbus, OH 43210

Janet Sheets
Baylor University
Moody Memorial Library
Box 6307
Waco, TX 76706

Diana Shonrock
Iowa State University
Parks Library Room 33
Ames, IA 50011

Sally R. Sims
University of Maryland
Architecture Library
College Park, MD 20742

Susan D. Skekloff
Helmke Library
Indiana University
2101 Coliseum Blvd. East
Fort Wayne, IN 46805

Fred E. Smith
Shippensburg University
Shippensburg, PA 17257

Jean Smith
University of California
Undergraduate Library
C-075-D
La Jolla, CA 92093

Shirley A. Snyder
Penn State University
Shenango Valley Campus
147 Shenango Ave.
Sharon, PA 16146

Virginia P. Sorensen
St. Cloud State University
Learning Resources
St. Cloud, MN 56301

Keith Stanger
Eastern Michigan University
University Library
Ypsilanti, MI 48197

Mary J. Stanley
IUPUI
University Library
815 West Michigan St.
Indianapolis, IN 46202

Edward D. Starkey
IUPUI
University Library
815 West Michigan St.
Indianapolis, IN 46202

Louisa Straziuso
Shawnee State University
940 Second St.
Portsmouth, OH 45662

Richard H. Swain
Cleveland State University
Library
1860 E. 22nd St.
Cleveland, OH 44115

Virginia Tiefel
The Ohio State University
1858 Neil Ave. Mall
Columbus, OH 43210

Nancy T. Totten
Indiana University Southeast
4201 Grant Line Rd.
New Albany, IN 47150

Joy B. Trulock
Valdosta State College Library
Valdosta, GA 31698

Carol Wall
Youngstown State University
William F. Maag Library
Youngstown, OH 44555

Mary Jane Walsh
Colgate University
Hamilton, NY 13346

Jeff Wanser
Library, Hiram College
Reference & Government Documents
Hiram, OH 44234

James E. Ward
David Lipscomb College
Nashville, TN 37204-3951

Janet K. Weir
Central Arizona College
Woodruff at Overfield
Public Services Library
Coolidge, AZ 85228

Victoria Welborn
The Ohio State University
B&Z Building, Room 200
1735 Neil Ave.
Columbus, OH 43210

Margaret R. Wells
SUNY at Buffalo
Undergraduate Library
Capen Hall
Buffalo, NY 14260

Cathryn E. White
University of North Carolina
Health Science Library (223H)
Chapel Hill, NC 27514

Marcia E. Whitehead
Boatwright Library
University of Richmond
Richmond, VA 23173

Marilyn P. Whitmore
University of Pittsburgh
207 Hillman
Pittsburgh, PA 15260

Marvin E. Wiggins
Harold B. Lee Library
Brigham Young University
Provo, UT 84602

Pamela S. Williams
Frostburg State College
Frostburg, MD 21532

Brenda J. Wilson
Courtright Memorial Library
Otterbein College
Westerville, OH 43081

Barbara Wilson-McNamee
Houston Academy of Medicine
Texas Medical Center Library
1133 M.D. Anderson Blvd.
Houston, TX 77036

Elizabeth J. Wood
Bowling Green State University
University Libraries
Bowling Green, OH 43402

Marie Turner Wright
IUPUI
University Library
815 West Michigan St.
Indianapolis, IN 46202

Henry York
Cleveland State University
Library-Social Science Reference
1860 E. 22nd St.
Cleveland, OH 44115

Vicki Young
Xavier University Library
3800 Victory Parkway
Cincinnati, OH 45207

Jane Zahner
Valdosta State College
Valdosta, GA 31698

Mark Zussman
Lansing Community College
419 N. Capitol Ave.
Lansing, MI 48901